Dire Moon Cartoons
(& More Performances)

Dire Moon Cartoons
John Sullivan

© 2021 John Sullivan

ISBN: 978-1-948712-62-0

Weasel Press
Lansing, MI
https://www.weaselpress.com

Contents:

Contents

Production Notes and Acknowledgements:

A early workshop version *Hey Fritz, Looks Like You Lost It All Again in the Ghosting* was performed for the Kansas State Theatre Forum. An excerpt, *"In Which Fritz Keeps a Brief, but Compulsory & Exceptionally Creepy Appointment with the Reich Minister of Propaganda,"* was published by the <u>BeZine</u> in an issue dedicated to theatre. *Dire Moon Cartoons* was produced by Theater Degree Zero (Directed by Jack Halstead - Tucson / Bisbee AZ). *Gray Sergeant* was published in <u>Prose Kitchen</u>. *Ishtar Over Berkeley* was published in <u>Anti-Heroin Chic</u>.

Please note that none of the scripts in this collection are formatted for live production – with the exception of *Ishtar Over Berkeley*. The other scripts may be used for production as radio plays – with a narrator/DJ for stage directions – commentary- asides - electronic enhancements. Live stage production versions of the scripts are available from the author.

Some notes on the work,

and the reasons why:

The story at the core of *Hey Fritz, Looks Like You Lost It All Again, in the Ghosting* stems from the moment in 1933 when German film auteur, Fritz Lang, was summoned to a meeting with Joseph Goebbels, Hitler's Reich Minister of Propaganda. Lang's newest film, *The Testament of Dr. Mabuse*, had been flagged, then banned by the Ministry of Public Enlightenment & Propaganda because, in the Minister's own words: "it showed how a cadre of dedicated criminals could overthrow the state by violence." But in Lang's framing of events, the deeper, unspoken crime was the deranged behavior of the mob's Boss Man / Big Bad Who in his film. Dr. Mabuse projected unmitigated malevolence and talked / carried himself like a high echelon NAZI. In Lang's telling, he sold his wife's jewelry that very night, and hopped on a train to Paris, eventually finding more permanent safety in California. In actuality, he left Berlin permanently four months later, but it's a good story, and it's his story, from his own lips, not ours.

Hey, Fritz ... spends a lot of time in Lang's head, in a dream state bordering on psychosis, long after the man, himself, was dead. His ruminations run the gamut of a career spanning his Expressionist / Noir beginnings in Germany through his major Hollywood studio years. In process, he encounters a number of former associates and/or rivals like Josef von Sternberg and Billy Wilder, two living artists and entertainers from our own era, Karen Finley and Bill Maher, and reunites, in a sense, with a former film collaborator, possibly an old flame, the international icon, Marlene Dietrich. Dietrich, Wilder and von Sternberg drop poop and a few *bon mots* on Hollywood mores, trade snarky taunts and ratchet up the coefficient of mutual contempt while Lang stands mostly apart and aloof – we're never sure exactly what he's thinking. Frank O' Hara is also part of the cast, mostly because his essay on *Personism* was so essential to writing this piece. Look closely and you'll find a quote or two from this Ur-text, coming straight out of his own mouth. All in all, it was a good move to invite him into the ensemble. His *joie de vivre* is infectious; his impact on the group gestalt, almost entirely positive. And he's not a bad actor, either.

But ultimately there's more going on here. Lang, the character, seems convinced that his evil creation, Mabuse, has escaped the film and still dogs him through dream after dream. Even dying doesn't seem to shake him; Mabuse sticks like a second skin or a disease contracted through exposure to the NAZI's. Perhaps his experience with the Reich's de-braining apparatchiks led him to realize – or at least consider - that artists have a deep moral responsibility for the images they make, ideas they birth and turn loose upon the world, and the company they keep. Lang, the true-enough human being, was fervently anti-Nazi after he left Germany, and worked with Bertolt Brecht on an anti-NAZI film, *Even Hangmen Die*, during his Hollywood years. It must have caused him no small measure of pain and shame that Hitler and Goebbels truly loved his work. And Leni Riefenstahl, the "docu-genius" behind *Triumph of the Will* and *Olympia*, claimed Lang as her most important artistic influence.

The **Dire Moon Cartoons** dredge up a lot of style and velocity - hubris, too, I reckon - from the storied history of cartooning: particularly old-school animated work from Warner Brothers and Walter Lantz Studios, and the pages of the original Mad Magazine. The frenetic action of Mack Sennett's Keystone Cops is also crucial to the mix, as is the testy / sometimes withering irony, a signature bit of that ancient Marx Brothers radio show, *Flywheel, Shyster & Flywheel*. Especially, in the "all-over-the-map" tenor and sting of the anarchic dialogue.

While these shortish 'toons are barely grounded in consensus reality – if at all - they are actually the most tightly plotted work in the bunch, and the logic behind their threads of events and character motivations is straightforward and, I hope, clear. But an audience, or reader, must suspend disbelief and accept the central premise that mice, red bugs and arcane humanoid characters like "Plunker's" and "Collapsible Tina's" do exist with real self-agency in this alternate reality. And they actually perform actions worth watching and extend their dialogic claws and powers of soliloquy to say words worth hearing.

I frame the Mouse van Gogh—star of *The Big White Chair*—as a true "Mouse of the People," much like Chaplin's heroic Tramp. Carlos Andrade grabs the essence of the original Tramp in his poem, *Song for That Man of the People, Charlie Chaplin*: a "vagabond whom the world has expelled, and yet [he] goes on living and clowning ... foiling hunger, dodging brutality, perpetuating love like a secret whispered in the ear of a common man [or woman] fallen in the street." I'd like to think the Mouse van Gogh partakes of and projects that same essence. And the feeling of that last scene where the Mouse communes on a trans-galactic level with her/his conceptual Angel Baby sources back to Chaplin's final gestures in *City Lights*. So precisely focused, so intense and so deeply quiet: it simultaneously hurts and opens the heart to signs and wonders. Probably the Tramp's most transcendent moment in a long line of gems. Dream on, Mouse, dream on: your day will surely come! In contrast, the stoically slogging *Gray Sergeant* and the poor, befuddled *Red Bug (aka Hoot Cootie)* are sad cases, indeed.

The Baby's Rookie Year strives to echo some of early Chris Burden's dire edge, vintage Vito Acconci's playful / banter-energy, and the unflinchingly honest, self-critical regard of Marina Abramovic. Hopefully, these currents shine through as feelings and tonal qualities. That said, the Rookie's story is not a script for / or commentary on a performance art piece but, rather, a piece of performed writing open to a variety of platforms for receiving and processing.

9

One of The Rookie's prime overt influences is Tim O'Brien's novel, *Going After Cacciato*. Rookie's episodic stream of events and experience, interpenetration of more or less real-world and the obviously not-so life-ways, looping (nearly snarling) threads of time / place / and character, and frequent jarring incongruities / probable impossibilities mirrors the world of *Cacciato's* funhouse / abattoir war. In O'Brien's endgame, an Asian woman, a refugee, (Sarkin Aung Wan) and an American GI (Paul Berlin) meet in an improvised "tribunal" space to deconstruct the deeply personal emotional damage and the cultural / political stakes in their conflicts with each other. But The Rookie's strange dialogue with the victims of his own violence and the oppressions of other more powerful actors is less specific. The conflicts, now, are almost planetary and the threats multiply sourced / many-pronged / of so many ideological stripes at once. Mirrored images / fluid time-streams / and focused-prophetic glossolalia are keys, here.

Naomi Wallace's *In the Heart of America* covers some of the same territory but my debt to her is totally different. Her remarkable / heartbreaking character, Craver Perry, opened my eyes to The Baby Rookie's possible true identity. It seems a lot of him is me. Or could have been. Or once was. I'm not so sure how this works, but it seems to. And her grim research on the lithe and clever gizmos of death, envisioned and devised by power, then visited on the weak (and in the way) to terrorize and subdue them: how it goes on and on. Craver's story re-opened my willfully shut eyes to the ways and means used by privilege – and my own privilege gets no pass here – to keep the cash flowing, to keep the lie cooking, to stay a'squat the top of the heap: way up there in the Catbird seat. *¡Solidaridad, Hermana!*

Footnotes to *The Rookie* are intended to give context and extend the scope of connections among readers, *The Rookie* and the rest of life. I hope no one is offended by this inclusion (or, possibly, intrusion?). Terror seems to come in so many fungible formats these days. And it may also be argued that it's all the "same as it ever was." Only the

10

hats and canes (think: uniforms / logos / action figures and bobble-heads) and formal choreography (think: tactical extravaganzas of newer Shocks & more deeply penetrating Awes) are different. Regardless, it seems some additional observations / opinions / ideas / judgments, or examples of their crying lack, might be necessary for the sake of roundness.

The pieces in this book – including the more or less self-evident *Ishtar Over Berkeley* – are all recombinant experiments: much like running gene sequences through CRISPR then reshuffling the results across species, or building synthetic life-forms, or pursuing time travel. Poetry, spoken word, and non-realistic / devised theatre are mutually-reinforcing, complementary forms, and the montage process jump-starts a cross-fertilization that often produces really interesting hybrids. I've never made that much of a distinction between poetic practice, performance and play-craft: they physically inhabit sound-scapes; they move within very similar technical parameters; they clearly embody the same bold spirit. And they all seem to be speaking out of the same mouth. Sometimes, all at once.

In Solidarity,
john Sullivan (*aka Da – Da – Da*)

Dire Moon Cartoons
(& More Performances)

John Sullivan

Hey Fritz, Looks Like You Lost It All Again in the Ghosting

Characters:

Fritz Lang (German Film Writer / Director)
Josef von Sternberg (another German Film Director)
Billy Wilder (American Film Writer / Director)
Frank O'Hara (American Poet / New York School)
Karen Finley (American Performance Artist)
Bill Maher (American Comic / anti-Pundit)
Marlene Dietrich (World Famous Film Icon, & Chanteuse)
Dr. Mabuse (Down & Dirty Character from Fritz Lang's Dr. Mabuse crime series, perhaps a proto-Nazi)
Dr. Joseph Goebbels (Nazi Minister of Information / Propaganda, perhaps a clone of Dr. Mabuse, or vice-versa)
Blind Jane (a Tiresius-like character, an aspect of Mabuse or Marlene Dietrich, or both)

Character Note: Josef von Sternberg and Bill Maher occupy the same body. Karen Finley and Billy Wilder occupy the same body. Marlene Dietrich, Dr. Mabuse, and, briefly, Blind Jane and Joseph Goebbels occupy the same body. This arrangement is often inconvenient. Fritz Lang and Frank O'Hara are out there on their own.

Setting: An interior: physical and mental

1. "Prologue: A Steady Stream of Bad-Bad Dreams"

(Film clips dance all over Fritz while he sits or they follow him like a spotlight as he moves around during his monologue. An actual 16 mm projector would be the best choppy, "funk-choogled" substrate for this stream of images from various *Mabuses*, or *Destiny, M, Hangmen* ... or even *Rancho Notorious*.)

(Fritz sits in Marlene / Mabuse's chair with head in hands and moans and speaks through the moaning. Listen carefully: it's hard to moan and speak in the same breath.)

Fritz:

Mabuse, I killed you, don't you remember that? Go back to the City of Smoke. *Raus meine kopf mit dir.*

(Pause.)

I said, get the hell out of my head, *böser Geist.*

(No movement, then it becomes obvious that – figuratively speaking - Fritz and his head are about to part ways. He speaks. He paces while he speaks. Sometimes he gestures like a drunken windmill, or holds his head like he's got a migraine, or points and wags his fingers like he's hectoring a ghost.)

Himmeldonnerwetter noch mal! It just doesn't work. No matter how long I stay dead, I seem to keep dreaming. I mean ... I know your hair grows and your fingernails, but I thought the eyelid movies stop when we unplug the protagonist and the audience leaves the show-house. Now I know the real score on that one. "What dreams may come, what dreams may come," indeed. Hamlet was right to worry.

Ow! There's that oily voice of Joseph Goebbels – droning on like a smug self-derangement tape – "Here is the man who will give us the Big Nazi pictures." You hear that too? (Taps on his skull.) Right inside here ... never goes away. And Leni Riefenstahl and their sick nincompoop of a Maximum Leader, mooning over my images of dominance and transfiguration – O *Destiny*, O my poor *Destiny* – and Riefenstahl even said: "Lang taught me how to make images of total submission so alluring that any flesh, anywhere will just give it up like a robot." I was in Los Angeles, then, eating lotus, sucking

16

skin, drinking in the sun, bobbing up and down in the surf like a postcard.

Leck meine arsh, I said; I unleashed *Der Testament das Doktor Mabuse* to show Europe what's what behind those brown shirts and goose-steppin' swastikas. I hunkered down, made an anti-NAZI film with Brecht, *Even Hangmen Die* – remember that one? – and waited for Hitler's *Götterdämmerung* to suck them all down into the sewer they made of Germany.

To them, I was just another useful ass-licker, kind of suspect, you know, half a Jew from *meine Mutti*, so they thought this *volte*-face was a fine joke on me ... it set me running from my old life, the language of my heart (now just a pervert's babble), from all the landscapes, all the skin I touched with images of need and desire, to Paris, before the fall, and then, to newer places. Tell you what: I never could outrun the pressure of those memories of Europa – right here, inside my head, lodged like a bullet - or finally dodge those regiments of dream-Gestapo. So I turned my back like the sad blue-angel of history and let the gusts of death blow past me. Or so I thought.

Look, I'm not a soldier. I came with all haste to America just to unplug my memory, and unclench and breathe deep like a California sun-king. My art was its own war. **(Pause.)** All the truth I ever knew.

(Pause). I did know that ... once. I remember I ... did ... that ...

(Fritz handles "dream images" with the light stream. He picks one out of the stream, holds it up into the light, inspects it, tosses it back, and washes his hands in the light while he talks. But this washing, while it may offer a fascinating *gest*, is ultimately futile.)

... but I couldn't shake my ghosts. I stayed plugged in, unreeling these dreams, these ... ghost faces ... these traces of lust, fears made flesh. They still suck on my brain like a popsicle. **(Pause.)** My own so "very monumental" contributions to the world's collective snooze.

**(Fritz discards the stream of images
and shakes his fingers to dry them.)**

Why is the half-life of these tiny bits of light so much greater than my own? Why can't I turn off the old meetings and greetings and leavings and betrayals and just sleep?
(Pause.) And just quietly unravel? I'm dead for God's sake, and these ghosts just walk in and give my shoulders a good shake whenever they / want to ...

(At / Frank O'Hara saunters on stage and walks over to his spot. He waves a whole-body "*HI, I see you too*," at Fritz.)

(Fritz points at Frank.) ... like that: Mr. Frank O'Hara who mocks my movies – "cold, metallic, spiritless ...," indeed – and then dogs my sleep like a hungry fly. **(Fritz flips off Frank.)** That's just for you and your stupid Personism. Poets should stick to words, only, and leave real images to the pros.

(Josef von Sternberg / Bill Maher arrives with his own ghost cortege and tidies up his spot with a handkerchief.)

Ah yes, von Sternberg, you poor lovesick bastard. And not a lick of substance. You chased Dietrich across two continents, abased yourself, erased yourself, and what did it net you? Thanks, but no. Goodbye. Call you later, maybe. Probably not. More probably, sinking slowly into memory sickness. Well at least the alter-ego you acquired has some real teeth.

**(Josef holds a Bill Maher poster-mask in front of his face
and lets loose a big YAWP!)**

18

Don't get feisty on me. Television is the ultimate zero. Soma, Demerol. A stream of images to use once, then toss. I have nothing to do with it.

(Karen Finley / Billy Wilder bounds into the space and solidly owns her / his spot.)

(Fritz laughs: not a pleasant laugh.) I know how you like your women, Billy. Quiet, mostly. Unassertive, all the time. An object with a few warm holes when you want it; an acolyte to feed your fire when you need to burn. How interesting: now you get to share your skin with ... Karen Finley?

(Karen grabs Billy's (her own) throat with her hands and throttles him.)

Whoa! Looks like you two need a good walk in the woods. Tell me, Karen, what the hell is performance art, anyway?

Of course, there's a few others. All stuck together in one hydra-headed beast that blurs and shifts from Dietrich to Goebbels, but always fades back to the source: Doktor Mabuse. They are all so slick and willful. So indulgent. Crawling like terrible questions. Spiraling inside, beyond the common laws of walls. Just don't hold your breath waiting for them to make the show. They all follow unique, very personal rhythms.

(Fritz takes a longer pause. He's going to tell us a secret and needs to know the space is a safe container.)

If I have to spend my eternity dreaming, I want my dreams to be at least as grand as my movies. Manichean, cataclysmic, Gog and Magog locked together, fang to claw to jowl, you know, something existential, something bloody grand, worthy of a *Magnifico*. Like me.

Instead, I get this *böse kinderspiel* full of wrangling, theft, and failures. *Dorftrottel*, all of them. I don't even want to see these people, ever again, but I seem to be stuck, cranking out chains of Dietrichs, Wilders, and von Sternbergs, decoding messages from a future I can't ever touch. They sound like echoes from my past but ... Karen Finley? Bill Maher? The messengers are so strange and different. And Frank O'Hara? *Was Zum Teufel?* And then, Mabuse, who should be dead ... I killed him. Remember? Always Mabuse, following my spoor, stalking me across infernal cities of smoke and blue light. *Scheisse*, I built that very set. But how did I grow this devil child? And why am I always ...

(Fritz walks while he chants to his personal start position. His walk and his words are a devotion. Or an obsession. Or what's the difference?)

... dreaming all my children back into being,
dreaming all my children back into being,
dreaming all my children back / into being
dreaming ...

(Fritz cut off abruptly (at /) by Josef's GO)
Josef:
Go

(Von Sternberg marches Center Stage with a bottle of Night Train. 2 beats later, Frank joins him. Frank grabs the bottle and takes a long pull.)

2. "Establishing Shot"

(Frank and Josef celebrate with their bottle of Night Train, but Frank is hogging the elxir. They are both well-schnockered and that is evident. Holding each other upright is a vital piece of the action. Fritz runs a steady silent inner monologue of lamentations,

and explores a gesture, suspiciously like *Sieg Heil*! He doesn't like it and his feelings - in deep conflict - are evident.)

Frank:

So I said to poor Fritz ... *mal aimé* ... *mal aimé* ... hey, you can't hurt me this way. Cuz' I care. You know what I'm saying? **(Pause. Pulls on the Night Train.)** So what's the dig, Joseffa? Why all the Fritzian pyrotechnics?

Josef:

It's Mabuse again. Always Herr Doktor Mabuse bearing down on him he says. Ever since / he ...

Fritz:

(At /. Fritz interrupts from a way off-center crouch. Way off center.)

Mabuse ... Mabuse ... a thousand eyes make a thousand testaments ... eh, Mabuse ... like a second skin ... when story stops the leak begins ... you hear me, Mabuse ... *Morder*...

Frank:

Whoa there, Tex! Nobody should have to experience anything they don't need to experience.

Josef:

Exactly. I hear you. Precisely.

Fritz feels the world – especially that terra incognita inside his own head – would be better off without Mabuse and his schemes.

(Josef grabs the Night Train from Frank and takes a pull of his own.)

Ever since he fled Berlin a few beats ahead of Dr. Goebbels, his nerves twitch like a little crazy bomb. He thinks Mabuse – and dead NAZI's, too - created a simulacrum from all that Mabuse footage. And now the Doktor stalks him. Well, that's what he thinks, anyway.

(Josef takes another long pull.)

(Frank grabs the Night Train Express bottle in mid-pull. The elixir within spills on Josef. They grapple. The grapple becomes a deep embrace: Frank kisses Josef hard on the lips, and more so. So how should Josef interpret Frank's move?)

Frank:

O that Fritz, what a jokester. No?
Hey Fritz, *mein schatzi:* you got snake lights and armies of Indras,
Metatron bloomin' in yer' belfry, and Archangels out the *tuchus*,
and little Kali-Yuga boys and all twelve Imams, and colonial shills
and all their friggin' henchmen percolatin' in yer' ol' brainpan?
Huh?

(Frank pulls away from Josef's tight grasp ... see, Josef is still not so very sure, here, but he's weighing his options. Frank drunk-dance tiptoes close to Fritz to do his final: "nyah-nyah-nyah.")

Frank:

Fritz is freaking. Fritz is freaking ... you know, kinda'-sorta' leaking
something out like ... you know, lost it all again in the ghosting.
Again. *Tu sabes*, huh?

(Fritz bellows and bleats. Frank high-tails it back to Josef.)

Fritz:

Hey ... you guys ... *verpiss dich* ... go on ... beat it, you ......you ... *halt maul* ... *arschlöchers!*

Josef:

(Josef moves to hold Frank, then he doesn't, then he does ... we have no idea, now, how this turns out.)

See Frank, you got him going. I don't know why the hell you have to say things like that.

22

He ain't gonna' mellow down easy and he's – for sure - gonna' blow his top and then, it's look out Broadway Babies and Goodnight Irene and Katy bar the door, you know: all that stupid common stuff you Americans are wont to say ...

Frank:
Well I'm just sayin': I hear you and I think he just popped the lock on his solitary wigbox. O-Mi-God! ...

Frank & Josef:
Uh-Oh, here comes Fritz ...

(Frank and Josef do an eloquent Mack Sennett exit: slippin and a'sliding, creeping and a'hiding with just the right sound f/x. Fritz runs after them: slow and syrupy, like he's bogged down hard in a frustrating dream. Which, in fact, he is.)

Fritz:
Go on, *raus mit dir*. Big mouths. *Scheisskopfs*. Scram. You gave it all away. *Abgefukt total, jetzt.*

(Frank and Josef become static – and apparently invisible, to Fritz – elements within the *mise en scene*. Fritz sniffs around them, pokes, prods but never seems to recognize their presence. He wanders the set, explores Marlene's makeup: applies some lipstick, eye shadow, blush. But he's not so very good at it: what a *payaso* he becomes! Now the video monitor Upstage Center-Left lights up. That gets his attention!)

(Video runs latest installment of *"Gossip Queens on Location."*)

3. "Gossip Queens on Location"

(Technical note: 1 pre-HD camera. Hand-held, used both as sound / image recorder and as an occasional character.)

23

(Establishing Shot: Zoom close-up of Marlene's leg up on a chair. The shot holds for a long take; after all, these legs are perhaps the most brilliant legs in the history of film or, at least, in the era of the Golden Age. Marlene swoops and swirls: this move becomes a riff, becomes a motif in her way of gliding through the set, with her signature cane. (*Morocco*, remember?) She moves in a circle through the space and comes back for a graceful stop at the chair: open position, head thrown back. Someone off camera yells: *Mach es wieder*. She places her leg back in position; she does the swoop and swirl motif again. In the middle of the sequence, a bullhorn announces: "20 seconds, you have 18 seconds to make, 15 seconds to make the appropriate response to, 12 seconds to make ... you have 10 seconds to ... 8, 7, 6, 5, 4, 3 ... Fritz Lang. Hey, *Schau hier*, Fritz Lang ... *passt auf*."

(Dietrich will be a mouthpiece for Fritz during this Q & A for the home audience. Fritz startles when he hears his name; Marlene's answers to his questions have an obvious effect on his very unstable physical mask, stage presence and core affect: descending to the level of a pathetic ouch-cube.)

Marlene / Mabuse

It's light, do you hear me, light is our natural human element. All my life I have lived through my eyes. We should have eyes all around our heads.

(Off-camera voice: *Mach es wieder!* You have 18 seconds to make the appropriate response to, 14 seconds to answer *die nächste frage* ... you have /...)

Marlene / Mabuse

Du bist blöd! I TOLD YOU: my movies penetrate the future from the past like ancient fish swimming in a sea of memory.

(Dietrich positions her leg on the chair to repeat her move. She begins her sweep and is interrupted:)

(Off camera voice: *nächste* ... you have 15 seconds to make an
appropri ... you have 12 seconds to make an ... /)

Marlene / Mabuse
AS I SAID: "the actor is the opposite of a scarecrow. BECAUSE:
The primary purpose of the actor is to attract not repel.
BECAUSE: the primary attraction of the theatre is carnal – OF-
THE-BODY – not of the mind." DID YOU GET THAT? So go see
what you're / gonna' do with it.

(At /: Karen walks in, like a thrall, a zombie, or someone recently
hit on the head with a brick. She speaks over Marlene / Mabuse's
last phrase.)

(Come to think of it, a zombie is entirely wrong for Karen's
intentions / motivations (or lack of them, perhaps). She seems
entirely, too focused. We think thrall is better, here: both "under
the spell" and transfigured, and very confused as to why.)

(It's also possible that Karen is merely faking it until she better
understands (or at least memorizes) the inner landscape of her
character or solves the satisfaction algorithms of her director.

Alternatively, she may be rummaging around in her own
warehouse for a physicality she can bear to carry. Let's keep an
open mind on this and not judge her as too tentative, or erratic.
Yet.)

Karen:
"I go inside. Conscious. I whisper, then I'm gone.
Like a ghost. I learn about it ..." ... *scheisse!* ... what the fuck is this
supposed to mean? Like, I need some ... I'm almost embarrassed to
say this old school Strasberg garbage, but I need some freakin'
motivation to believe I'm really saying this shit. Would anyone,
anywhere believe anyone face-to-face who said ... well ... this too,

listen to this *kvatch*. "No, she says to him, because a knife is found somewhere, maybe borrowed, a cut cannot be magic" ... I mean is this is or is this not *abgefukt total*?

(Now Karen and Marlene / Mabuse share a gesture, together.
Their speech and movements recreate the feeling of a highly
charged dream. The exact charge is difficult to pin: this is a
different species of dream than we normally encounter.)

(During this gesture, Marlene reconfigures her iconic costume
(keep thinking, Morocco!) to more and more re(a)ssemble the
form, visage and demeanor
of Dr. Mabuse.)

Marlene / Mabuse
Karen, it's so close now. Karen, I'm losing my shape.
I'm losing this whole painting.
Are you here to kill me, or to spare me? Karen?

Karen:
Look, I have no idea why I must open myself to other selves,
like this, over and over.
I just do it.
I learn about it later.

Marlene / Mabuse:
Karen, are you there yet?
Touch me, without talking ...
Stay parallel to words
But don't forsake them. Either.
Karen, are you warm enough to blast off the mask?
Karen?

(Marlene positions Mabuse ½ mask over her face,
completes the transformation to Dr. Mabuse.)

26

(Off-camera voice: *Mach es wieder!*)

Karen:
What part?
Me talking, or this? (Holds up script.)

(Two signs appear. They both point to Dr. Mabuse with arrows.
One reads: Dr. Mabuse. The other reads: *böser Geist.*)

(Camera zoom on Mabuse / Marlene. Catch the flashy swastika
and stained neck bandage. And how the ½ mask complements the
overall *gestalt.* Closing shot: Mabuse / Marlene lips:
(s)he blows a sweet kiss into the lens.)

(Now our Gossip shoot is a wrap, though someone with a wise
head once said that "Gossip is all the people read / heed / need
anyway and, ultimately, it's all that's true as well." Yes, no, maybe
so? But, now, back to the embodied part.)

4. "The Water Cure"

(Karen / Billy appears from wing, suitably medical, appropriately
rubberized, to conduct a water cure therapy session with Fritz.
She takes him gently by the arm
and leads him over
to the therapeutic basin.)

Karen / Billy:
Mr. Lang, it's time for your water cure again.
This time, stay under as long as possible.
We want to drive all the ghosts out through your ears and your
nose. You want to get rid of all those ghosts, no?
Especially that bad Oscar, Dr. Mabuse.

(Karen / Billy pushes Fritz down into the basin and holds her hand on his neck. If Fritz raises his head, Karen / Billy allows him to gulp down a breath before she pushes his head back underwater.)

Have some faith, Mr. Lang, this really is more
like a prayer than babble from a ghost.
See: you breathe, you close your eyes,
You go inside, conscious.
Strict, rigorous, disciplined
A prayer of your perfect attention.
Maybe it's a lever of transcendence.
Maybe you'll learn about it later, no?

(Karen / Billy lifts Fritz out of the water by his hair. She speaks to him, plays with him, rubs salt into the wound left by his passage out of childhood. Like Big Sister back from the Corps.)

Mr. Lang, you've gotta' know these things take time.
If you want to blast a wolfish residue like Mabuse
right outta' your guts
or reignite an old torch for the Blonde Venus –
O *mein liebschen*
O (sings) *"My Lily of the lamplight"* –
her very own self, well then:
You gotta boogie through a gauntlet of pain balloons
And scary ectoplasms in full float
Like the whole damn drift of history.
Isn't it exciting Mr. Lang?
C'mon grin: let's see some lips and teeth.
FYI: my name is Karen Finley, I'm a famous
performance artist and I do so love
your very famous movies, especially the part in Metropolis
where Dr. Rotwang grabs Maria and lurches down into the bowels
of the city with all this steam and shit leaking this way and that
way and then that other part
where Our Lady of Submission, (Most Abject), bares / her ...

28

**(At /, Karen / Billy scopes Mabuse / Marlene
waltzing into plain view)**

... Whoa-weee!
That which shackles change dances right toward us.
And this is not the story of a true star.
No more.

5. "A Talking Cure for Fritz"

**(Karen / Billy dries off Fritz. Mabuse / Marlene floats through the
playing space in a passionate waltz with Fritz's Posey-vest restraint.
Mabuse / Marlene carries his cane in the crook of one arm.
(Morocco, again: we just can't kick that rhythm, no?) His / her
limp is evident throughout the dance.)**

**(Mabuse / Marlene approaches Fritz
and Karen / Billy.)**

Mabuse / Marlene:
(To Karen / Billy.)
Does he know?

Karen / Billy:
He knows.

Mabuse / Marlene:
Oh, he knows does he?

Karen / Billy:
Yeah, yeah. He really knows.
(Pause.)
But he's n-o-t talkin'.

(Karen / Billy and Mabuse / Marlene truss Fritz into his Posey.
Mabuse / Marlene dismisses Karen / Billy and K-B becomes
Mabuse's chair. Frank and Josef, no longer merely sight gags, sneak
back to their spots as bona fide observers. After all, how could we
guarantee truth in our theatre without objective eyes on the
inside? Maybe they're tweeting their followers while they watch?
Mabuse / Marlene begins a talking cure session with Fritz.)

Mabuse / Marlene:
Approach me child. Or are you my father?
We must fill your pain balloons with blah-blah,
Blah-blah-blah-blah.
First question: are you primed to dine and clang?

Fritz:
What?
(Turns away) I don't know. How should I know?
Why are you scaring me *zeit-schaten*?

Mabuse / Marlene:
**(Long sigh: the dying pain balloon
expends its spirit.)**
The prisoners forget so much.
Too often, they refuse so much.
(Directly to Fritz:)
Face me, father.
You know: skinny blood shadow and all
Will never full-belly be, again.

Karen / Billy:
(As talking chair:)
Too many skull-mates don't trust their instincts, no more ...

Josef:
and also, and to boot, no blue-blonde

30

inflictor angel ...

Frank:
all tapt' out and fly ...

Josef:
gonna' bop-hammer ...

Frank:
That fine, inflected spilt brain's too long gone
to signify.
Woo-wee!

Mabuse / Marlene:
(Signifyin' like a for real Pontiff: "bless you boys" and CUT the
Crap. Fritz is directly in front of Mabuse / Marlene. M / M
signals kneel and Fritz kneels.)

(To Fritz:)
You know I love you, but you've gotta' be a man, son.
Father? Whatever.

Fritz:
But Mom ...

Mabuse / Marlene:
I'm not a Mom.

Fritz:
I'm not a man.

Marlene / Mabuse:
No sweetie, you're not.
But all you really need to get there is a new set of ears.
(M / M lets loose a magnificent yawn.)
You blah-blah-blah so much.

31

People who blah-blah-blah so much wear out their own ears.

Fritz:
(Cups his ears.)
Now I can't hear?
I suppose next I can't talk?
I can't put forth any defense to / ... 'splain my

Mabuse / Marlene:
(At /:)
Oh *Halt maul*, yourself. Now you listen to me.
When you look for your own ears again, you'll find nothing but
useless holes. So now it's time for these ...

**(M / M attaches new ears to Fritz's head, so that he can wire back
into the cosmic sensorium. And also hear and do what he's told to
do. These ears are made to both attract and repel, depending on
the biases of the beholder. Sort of a hybridized version of Mickey
Mouse and Nosferatu. A pleasant enough shape, but with a
leathery and barbed texture, almost preternaturally prickly. These
new ears won't do much for Fritz's social standing among
Hollywood auteurs. But at this juncture
that hardly matters, does it?)**

Marlene / Mabuse:
(To all the others.)
Start the *maschina, apparatchikis*. This is all way too tame.
It's time to pile some darkness onto this bad animal.

**(M / M rises and Karen / Billy, no longer a chair, becomes one of
the *apparatchiki*.)**

Some bumps and jolts, strategically delivered
swift and sure
til he says *no mas*
til a whole world of coma ain't conscience enough for him

with me inside, way-tickin'.
My verdict is this angel is too so very lame
For a mere talka-talka-talkin' cure.

(Mabuse / Marlene nudges Fritz center / forward with his foot.
Mabuse beats time with his cane as the others chant
The Mad Town Jump Rope Chant.)

(Frank, Josef / Bill and Karen / Billy swing the rope and / or clap
time for Fritz's therapeutic game. Fritz is a klutz and doesn't do a
good job inside this action. He doesn't like it either and the others
have to keep him on track.)

6. "Dig the Mad Town Jump Rope Chant"

"Mad Town Jump Rope Chant":
(Frank, Josef and Karen sing: in unison and, alternately,
as separate voices in call & response.)

Last night
The night before
Twenty four shooter boys at my door
I was born in a moving van
I was born in a garbage can
I was born in a frying pan
Can you guess how old I am?
Little Miss B all dressed in blue
Died last night a quarter to 2
Before she died she said this stuff
Better run fast, better run far
Better run better or you're gonna' get snuffed
Doktor, Doktor: bizz-buzz-booze
Cop me a angel witha' alligator shoes
Doktor, Doktor: bizz-bazz-buzz
Cop me a angel witha' alligator fuzz

33

Mushroom-skyburn make me high
Bury my brain in the big blue sky
Hold my head and shake my face
Bury my body in the Maybe Place
Ouch me, shank me, feed me lead
Bury me now
Bury me then
Bury me later when I wake up dead.

(Fritz abruptly discontinues his therapy. Now, he'll get a big fat AMA on his paperwork. If and when he's ever discharged.)

Fritz:
Halt, halt, halt. Es ist Verruckt!
I came her to lose a ghost, not to be one.
What are you doing to me?

Karen / Billy:
... mommy's dolly, mommy's dolly, mommy's dolly ...

Frank:
He plays too damn good for his own good, yeah ...

Josef / Bill:
Tell you what: he makes dat mouf' rubba' burn...

Karen / Billy:
He eats gobs and gobs of that ol' graveyard stew!

Frank:
Fuckin' sweet, says he.
He thinks it tastes like fuckin' ambrosia?

Josef / Bill:
Ahhs-ville, indubitably. What a foo!

34

Fritz:
(Roars:)
I came here to rewrite my memories.
I came here to abolish, absolve, abjure all the friggin' mysteries
laid upon me by fate and destiny.
And by that one! **(Points to Mabuse.)**
I want a better history right here, right now ...

**(Josef hands Fritz the Night Train Express. Fritz takes on it,
catches himself in mid-reach for it...)**

... and you give me an eraser.
Who in *Holle* are you all?

Karen / Billy:
I'm the little sweet meat who lives in the attic ...

Frank:
... I'm the little mole with my feet in the heat ...

Josef:
We're your children.
All of your children.
Dragon's Tooth Children.

All:
... ain't no lack of us, see?

Karen / Billy:
Back home again, you hip-wicked Daddy!

**(Karen / Billy, Josef / Bill and Frank now behave like henchmen on
the payroll. They hold him up by his collar and grill him about his
relationship to Mabuse. They are looking for bomb-proof
causality, not mere association.
Of course, all of this rigmarole may be a ruse.)**

35

Josef:
(Points at Mabuse who arches toward them
sniffing like a bird dog but doesn't move.)
Him. Over there. We don't like him either.
Did you invent him?

Fritz:
I don't know.
At this point, I don't care.
Whatever you say.

Josef:
I said, did you invent him?

Frank:
Or did he make you?

Fritz:
So that's it. All my nasty little bugs back to feed at the source.
Scher dich zum Teufel!

(M / M lets loose another virtuoso yawn. Playing Pontiff, yet
again, M / M signals the crew to drop characters
and return to their respective spots.)

7. "In Which Fritz Keeps a Brief, but Compulsory & Exceptionally Creepy Appointment with the Reich Minister of Propaganda"

(Video stream pops on: clips from *The Testament of Dr. Mabuse* or
Metropolis or *Destiny* make a back-drop. Perhaps, also, something
from *Morocco*, no?)

(Fritz narrates the central story embedded in (in fact, actually responsible for) his staged story, his marginally effective therapeutic process, the fountainhead of all his demons, self-described as "sucking at his brain like a popsicle." Here, he has permission to stride, flail, gesture, rail, and etc. Such is the stuff of really bad dreams. Or recurrent PTSD.)

(During the narration process Mabuse reverts to Marlene using the same makeup Fritz applied to his own face earlier. If she loses her place, she can always look up and revive her inspiration with her own "Amy Jolly" image in Sternberg's film. 2 beats. I never said *Morocco*.)

(Very muted, almost subliminal audio track: one possible suggestion, Kraftwerk's *Fun, Fun, Fun on the Autobahn*. Another possibility: Peter Lorre's obsessional-confessional murder theme from *M*.)

Fritz:
So then I invented the next Mabuse: *Das Testament des Dr. Mabuse*.
And I said: now I am finished. I am killing him.
I put into the mouth of a mad killer all the NAZI slogans.
Schluss! Aus! Fertig!

(Fritz and Frank do their own version of call and response during this narration. Leave the full-embodied narrative to Fritz, Frank. Remember, poets are supposed to stick to words.)

Frank:
A container of images, actions, punctured like skin

Fritz:
When the picture was finished, some henchmen of Dr. Goebbels came to the office.
They threatened to forbid the movie.
That's rich, I thought. I laughed out loud.

37

I was very short with them.
If you think you can forbid a picture by
Fritz Lang ... Fritz Lang, Fritz Lang,
Fritz ("Freakin'") Lang,
and I know you know what that means in Germany.
So ... if you think you can do that ...
well, just go right ahead with your stupid plan.
And so they did.

Frank:
And so this next virus achieves its own release

Fritz:
I was ordered to go see Dr. Goebbels.
My "interview" was held in the new Ministry of Propaganda.
It was frightening and very disagreeable.

Frank:
Dial me up a lens against

Fritz:
You go down long, wide corridors of gray flag-stone, etc.
Your steps scuff against the stone and echo, etc.
As you come around the corner – any corner will do –
you meet these hard men in pairs and clusters.
They sneer and play with their lugers, and shivs, etc.

Frank:
Missionary myopia, down for a little fucking vertigo?

Fritz:
You begin to sweat.
You come to a first desk. A second, then a third desk.
And finally, a little room where they say:

Frank, Karen / Billy and Josef/
(with Bill Maher chomping in the wings) all shout:
You! Wait here!

Marlene / Mabuse
(Repeats the command, as if she were addressing a small child,
or an addled, possibly dissociated sleepwalker.)

Ja. Ja. Ja. Du wartest hier, Süße.

Fritz:
Later, a door opens on a long, spacious office
of burnished hardwood.
At the very end of the long office is Dr. Goebbels.
He smiles.

Frank:
Pleasure or avoidance, inscape or erasure: unity, again,
but only for the Pure.

Fritz:
And so he says to me:

(Bill Maher / Josef goosesteps upstage and stops next to Fritz. Bill
Maher speaks to the audience in an exceedingly lame, "Hogan's
Heroes" sit-com German accent. Perhaps, the actor speaks
through a Bill Maher tour poster featuring Bill Maher's face.)

Bill / Josef:
(To audience:)
Meine damen und herren ...
(To Fritz:)
Mein herr, look, I am terribly sorry but we had to confiscate this
picture. / It ...

39

Karen / Billy:
(At /. As Karen:)
Bill, do you have any clue how dumb and corny
and patronizing that sounds?

**(Pause. Karen is pent up and primed to tangle with Bill Maher.
They have some unpleasant history which will soon be manifested.
Something like this:** *"du bist wirklich der Beweis, dass nicht alles was
zwei Backen hat, ein Gesicht sein muss!")*

This act is supposed to be a representation: BUT what you're doing
isn't ART.

Bill / Josef:
Karen, this Schtick, in case your coloring book is shy a few dots, is
not about ART.
And while we're on the subject: explain to the rest of us squares
how this
low-rent, shuck & jive-ass séance could ever be ART.

**(Bill pauses to enhance his extra-daily technique
and dilate his stage presence.)**

Or what we are missing when they, like, saw a cow in half on stage
...
and then that's ART, too, I suppose?

Karen / Billy:
Well. Let's go to Michelangelo with, I think ... there the big dead
ART is Jesus,
the cadaver on the cross for the "Pieta" which is ...

Marlene / Mabuse:
**(Short (but not dismissive), decisive (but out-of-love with power),
imperious, irresistible, and totally inevitable: the** *Blonde Venus*

accepts a loathsome role to move the action forward. What a
trouper!)

I'll do "Dr." Goebbels. I knew the man once ... and, well,
he had strong opinions on life and death, art, and decency.
(Marlene now channels Joseph Goebbels:)
Look, I am terribly sorry, Mr. **(Pause)** ... uh - Fritz Lang?
But there was NO choice; we had to confiscate this picture.
It was the ending we didn't like.
A picture such as this must have another ending.
The criminal's insanity is not punishment enough for his crimes.
He must be destroyed by *das Volk*.

Fritz:
He didn't say anything about the real reasons:
hare-brained NAZI philosophy and NAZI gutter-buzz words,
unmindful stupidity and willful NAZI ignorance
pouring from the mouth of an insane criminal:
totally addicted to mind control, torture, murder
and seizures of passion.
I could only think: how do I get out of here?
I wanted to get my money out of the bank.
I wanted to run.

Frank:
X'ed, dist' and dumped: and who's next on the slab?

Fritz:
Finally, he said to me:

Marlene / Mabuse
(as Joseph Goebbels:)
Der Führer has seen your pictures and he proclaimed:

Karen / Billy:
(Just briefly, as *Führer der Nation*:)

41

Fritz:

Yes. **(Pause.)** Here is the man, indeed.
The man who is supposed to give us the great NAZI pictures.
And he splays his arms out: blooming, like a belladonna flower.
No remedy in this one, no way, just a crass assassin.
And he wants to know what I have to say to all this.

Frank:

Give me Vertigo or give me Demerol?

Fritz:

So I said, I am tickled-pink, Herr Minister.
What could I say? I said YES, YES to everything.
But at one point, I also said to myself:
This is the last moment you can ever be sure
of getting out of Germany, alive.
And when can I ever stop ...

Karen / Billy and Frank and Josef / Bill:

... dreaming all my children back into being
dreaming all my children back into being
dreaming all my children back into being

(Fritz goes back to his original position at "GO." His entire being now focuses on tactics for disremembering these persistent dreams and the "children" that steer them.)

8. "You Can Look But You Better Not Touch"

(Marlene finishes her makeup and final costume adjustments. She signals Karen to approach and together they reenter their unusual dream state.)

**(If you haven't seen it yet, please refer
to Gossip Queens. Marlene tags Karen...)**

Marlene (no Mabuse, here):
(To Karen:)
You're it. I'm all yours, *schatzi.*

**(Video pops on: streaming clips of *The Blue Angel*,
The Devil is a Woman and, of course, *Morocco*.)**

**(Marlene and Karen morph beyond their previous gesture. They
slowly cover the stage in a dance of approximate love
and actual menace.)**

**(Karen speaks all of the next with exception of bold face
interjections by Josef.)**

She's lying in the cold yellow light
Says the actor
stretched out straight
her breasts outside the mass of her body
beautiful, numinous
of pale marble
of pure light

If she spoke
Says the actor
She would say:
If our affair were acted in the theatre
An actor would come to the brink of the river
The lip of a dark well
The edge of a deep canyon
Of pure light, and blinding
But very close to you
And to me beside you

43

But that actor would look only at you.
And speak only for you.
He would speak as you would speak if you had spoken
Slowly, and quietly
Eyes turned starward
Reading it all off the ceiling
Of some literary text

But through it all
A text, from which he was constantly distracted
And the text, stretched tight
Until it almost snaps,
Distorted by the effort
Of ignoring
The other woman
- the ME -
And her presence on the stage

Marlene / Mabuse:
Between you and me there is a murder.

**(Josef morphs back into Bill Maher.
Marlene / Mabuse goes back to her chair.)**

Bill / Josef:
Oooh-Kaaaren: there's an exhibit going on
right now in Manheim Germany
where they have these cadavers preserved in plastic
in different
- But Real! -
These are real human cadavers
- Dead Humans, you know! -
they have like a guy with skin peeled off
and he's playing chess.
Chess, Karen, like with Hannibal the Cannibal

Karen / Billy:
Sounds like the kind of art I like, Bill.

Bill / Josef:
That's why I brought it up.

Karen / Billy:
Did that skinned man give you a boner, Bill?

Bill / Josef:
Should the government fund my boner?

Karen / Billy:
Only if it's a *decent* boner, Bill.

**(Karen / Billy and Bill / Josef close up shop abruptly, spin
on their heels (a nice Prussian military spin, perhaps), and
march back to their spots.
Bill Maher morphs back into Josef.
Josef retrieves cordage, walks back to Marlene with Frank.)**

9. "Stuck in the Middle With You."

**(Josef and Frank tie cordage around the wrists and neck of
Marlene. (Loosely, this is merely symbolic.)
Josef speaks to and of Marlene as they work.)**

Josef:
You may as well give up on Fritz, my friend.
He's hopelessly addicted to his own paranoia.
His violence without action, his lust without affect.
Gott in Himmel, the critics say such things about us –
Especially Fritz after M.
Great film but a bad career move, and Lorre,
Ick! Such a nasty smelling little

45

crypt beetle if ever there was. But, you know,
at least his paranoia is entirely his own.
Which is more than he can say about Mabuse.
Or this wonder I gave to the world.

Frank:
(Also tying, but mostly framing the shot
and beaming.)
So you say you did, Josef.
(Aside:) "There goes love's life-giving vulgarity, again."

Josef:
Geographies of care: all these tiny wrinkles
spread across her forehead.
And these clown-lines radiating from her mouth.
Superfluous on such a handsome face, don't you think?
I told her not to think too deeply.
But she did, just to spite me.
And then she became more interesting to me
than her image.

Frank:
"You're flattering yourself into thinking
That what you're experiencing is yearning," pod'ner.

(They finish and step back from the newly refurbished
icon. Marlene lights up a Lucky Strike and falls into a slow
marionette's riff on her classic physicality. Hard and
pointy, passive and lush, warm to a point, predatory, ultra-
world weary, calculating, aloof and detached
from the effect of her affect on all of us.
Please circle the nuances of effect / affect
that you would most like to see.)

46

(Joseph morphs back into Bill Maher. Bill and Karen
continue their barb-fest on performance art, the 1st
Amendment laced with smack-talk.)

Bill / Josef:
(To Karen:)
You're a great champion of the 1st Amendment, right?

Karen / Billy:
Yes. You know I am, Bill.

Bill / Josef:
Would you want a nation where
They don't recognize the 1st Amendment?

Karen / Billy:
I don't feel it's recognized here.
I lost my suit. So I don't feel it's here.

Bill / Josef:
You can go into any club in L.A.
And they'll hire you to do your act.

Karen / Billy:
This is not about my act.
This is about my suit.

Bill / Josef:
And your suit wasn't about the 1st Amendment, really.
Your suit was about doing / your ...

Karen / Billy:
(at /:)
I'd be happy to get into my suit right now.

Bill / Josef:
Now I'd really like to get into your suit.
(Canned laughter.)

Karen / Billy:
I am really mad at you, but I guess I will talk
about my indecent behavior.

Bill / Josef:
Karen, talking to you just makes my mouth happy.
Let's take a commercial, and we'll come right back
to get deeply into your indecent behavior.

Karen / Billy:
I am really mad at you, really mad at you, really ...

**(Bill's misogynist repartee finally punctures Karen's
structure, as Karen Finley. She gob-smacks herself,
sputters, and erupts as –
What? Who? - Billy Wilder?? Whoa!)**

Billy / Karen:
(Speaking Billy's words in Karen's voice *just this once*:)
"In real life, most women are stupid ... and so are persons –
so-called persons – who write biographies
of Hollywood celebrities."

10. "Destry Rides Again"

**(Billy Wilder / Karen explodes into the scene, annexing
every cubic centimeter of space, presuming
all prerogatives of his gender
(circa 1950s, though 1590s might work just as well)
and his leveraged status as a major industry player.
He strides directly toward Marlene
and immediately begins his customary grope.)**

(Billy / Karen now speaks directly in the voice of Billy
Wilder. Think Brillo pad marinated in stale Budweiser
from last night's session.
Maybe a couple of cigarette butts,
and a used fit, to boot.)

Billy / Karen:
(To Sternberg (or, perhaps, just for his benefit).
How subtle can this guy be, after all?)
Love ya', Love ya, Love ya', baby.
(Stops in mid-grope:)
What the Fuck!
(Over his shoulder to Josef:)
Hey Sternberg, this model's got no action parts.

(Remember, Blonde Venus is now a marionette. Lucky for
Billy Wilder: you notice,
his face is still intact.)

So what the fuck good is this model?

(Frank editorializes with his own personal system of
imagistic semaphore.)

Josef / Bill:
Obviously you need more blood in your brain.
You don't even know your heart is asleep.
My heart is a lens that holds
all her psychic imprints.
Action parts, indeed.
All you do is animate kitschy-kooey snapshots.

Billy / Karen:
And all-you-do-is-masturbate-

49

With-your-precious-psychic-imprints-
In-your-palm-with-your-pud.
**(Big Breath: Billy gulps up all the air in the "room."
And he knows it.)**
Ooo-Wee, that felt good. Hey, get real, Joe.
My *dupa* makes more sense than your bloody *Corazon*.

Josef / Bill:
Ha! You don't even know how to shoot a simple kiss.
To shoot a kiss on film: a lens
must focus on the ear, a mirror, etc.
Any other object but the actual lips
will state the difference between one nose
and the other nose
in absolute terms.

Frank:
And irons out all the distortions, too!

(Go back to your silent semaphore, Frank. Please?)

Billy / Karen:
Kiss, huh?
So you want to kiss it?
OK, OK, I'm an obligin' kinda' guy.

**(Billy / Karen grabs Josef by the neck and carefully
positions his mouth against Dietrich's. Like (s)he's
assembling a delicate tongue and groove joint (or
composing a shot). This *mensch* is an artiste, no?)**

Billy / Karen:
There ... that's the kiss you've always wanted,
huh, Joe?
Hold that tongue against that other tongue ... hold it ...
hold it ... and there you go.

50

Ooo-Wee, it drives you crazy don't it?
Am I right, Joe?

(Billy releases the necks of "his actors."
Josef is traumatized and scurries back to his Go spot.
Marlene calmly drags again on her Lucky Strike.)

(All this action agitates Fritz. He stirs, sputters, puts his
ear down to the floor sweeping back and forth
for the faintest sound.
There! He has it.)

Fritz:
*Polizei ... polizei ... sen ... soriert durch die bullen ... listen ... die
bullen ... passt auf ...*
(Fritz knocks on the floor with his fist
and pulls back like a spooked horse.)

Billy / Karen:
What's the deal, Fritz?
Are you just that wigged, are you really that wired?
(Pause, as Billy Wilder develops another
diabolical idea for raising the ante
in this gabby wrangle with his friends.)
Or are you just that jealous?
(Pause. This is gonna' be some kind of fun.)
Yeah ... that's it.
You and Jo-Jo hustled the same merchandise.
(Pause.)
Guess that kissy stuff got to you, no?

(Billy W / Karen strides toward Fritz,
grabs his collar and hoists him up.)

Billy W / Karen:

**(Like: it's gonna' hurt but this
is for your own good, Fritz:)**
You're coming undone. Fritz.
Get your shit together.
Hollywood's been good to you.

**(Drops him, strides away, moving, gesturing, talking with
Mac-10 level manic energy.)**

Yeah, I can still see the marquee, *Destry Rides Again*.
A Fritz Lang ...
a freakin' Fritz Lang western, for Christ's sake.
Starring Marlene Magnifica, as tough but true but also
kinda' easy if you got what it takes, if you got what it needs,
if you catch the drift of my history. here...

**(Pause. Gathers her / his presence to wax his
Billy Wilder version of rhapsodic.)**

O Marlene, you saloon floozie extra-ordinary,
And ... and also starring ... also ... that other guy?

Fritz:
I didn't make that picture. That was Marshall's movie.
I made *Rancho Notorious*, instead.
Dietrich's character was like Frenchie, you know,
just like in *Destry*, but older, now.
She was Altar Keane in my movie.
And she resented, in fact actively resisted
going gracefully into that OLDER category.
Instead, she became younger and younger and ...
... it was hopeless ...
... by the end of the picture
we didn't speak to each other any more.

Billy / Karen:

(Uses Marlene the marionette to illustrate:)
Blonde, bejeweled, leggy and kinda' still handsome.
Destry Rides Again: you gotta' sorta' love it.

Fritz:
**(Advances on Billy / Karen: like Mike Piazza moved on
Roger Clemens during the famous "broken bat incident.")**

No. Wrong again, *meine dumme kleine freund-schen.*
Rancho Notorious was about Lust, Hate,
Murder and Revenge.
It's true: I tell you every passing year
is a threat to a woman like Altar Keane.
But Dietrich was even more attractive than 20 years before.
It was so damn frustrating.
All the time we worked on Rancho Notorious
she would suggest this and recommend that
saying, "von Sternberg did it that way."

**(Josef takes a deep bow. Fritz goes through "rage of the
mad scientist" out the other end into mild amusement.
Hey, he's Fritz Lang.)**

But THIS was my picture.
Not his.
I did it all my way. My way!
In the end, she caught a bullet meant for her lover.

Billy / Karen:
Whoa, there, cowpoke!
Rancho Notorious ... hmm ... If I was you, Fritz,
Hell, I'd stick with *Destry.*

**(Billy / Karen spins to face Fritz. You know, he really likes
that spin: it feels good, even kidlike,
and it probably makes a good visual.**

53

**So he spins again. He points to Josef and who knows: his
finger may be a gun in their respective imaginaria.
Josef cowers and cringes.)**

You want to end up like him?
Down the ol' poop-chute of oblivion.
Some say she drove him crackers n' nanners,
crackers and nanners!
(Like the crooner on the radio:)
Drove insane by that sweet, sweet jelly-roll!

**(Reading Josef, now, the holy writ
of Hollywood excommunication:)**

Who the hell knows you now in this town, Joe?
In this town, you just remember endings.
You never did get that, did you Joe?
Nothing but endings.

**(Billy / Karen strides to Marlene marionette
and stands behind her.)**

Mira, Joe. This is how you do an ending.
This is a *Foreign Affair*, my man.
This is the soul of *Sunset Boulevard*.
(Direct from the sludge pits of American id.)
A real trouper talkin'.

**(Billy / Karen works the Marlene marionette
with the cords tied by Josef and Frank.)**

(Billy / Karen (as the Marilyn), still talking:)
"... and they ask me, they say: Marilyn
with a full life in pictures,
and a full life in every other place, too, they say
Marilyn, what do you have to be proudest about?

54

So I look into their eyes - like this ...
(Don't forget this move, Marlene)
and I say, well, everything, just everything ...
I'm proudest of everything ..."

(Marlene / Mabuse (still the marionette?) rubs Billy /
Karen's hand carefully against her face, and then bites
down hard on his / her fingers. S(h)e flicks her ashes on his
head while he hops and howls. 5 beats: they freeze in mid
flick / mid hop / mid howl.)

Frank:
(Waltzes over to Josef and overflows onto him.)

"And what can we expect of Joseph Cotton puzzling
and Orson Wells puzzled, and Delores del Rio
eating orchids, and Gloria Swanson
reclining and Jean Harlow reclining, and
wriggling, and Faye Raye reclining and wriggling
and singing, and Elizabeth Taylor blossoming,
yes, unto thee ...
(Aside:) This is getting good ...
(Pause:)
What can we expect? Why everything ... just everything."

(Pause. Waves at the audience
like a true star.)

But we won't get it.

(Marlene / Mabuse and Billy / Karen disengage from their
long moment. Marlene / Mabuse reassembles her iconic
costume. (I'll bet you thought we would refer to Morocco,
again.) S(h)e walks deliberately toward the wing but never
quite out of sight. She becomes visibly older with each step.
Billy / Karen watches her and rubs his / her fingers.

B/K moves back to Karen's GO spot.)

Josef:
(Uncorks a new bottle of Night Train Express.)

Frank, sometimes you truly elude me.
**(Josef takes a strong pull off the bottle
and hands the bottle to Frank.)**
Here, I suggest we toast the *mise en scene.*

Frank:
(Toasts and talks:)
"The heavens, too, operate on the star system.
It's a divine precedent we perpetuate.
Roll on reels of celluloid,
As the great earth rolls on."

(All present return to their GO spots.)

11. "Choose a History, or You Can Just Perform One"

**(Marlene / Mabuse turns back toward us as Blind Jane.
This character owes something to Yeats,
something to Sophocles, and something else to Moon Dog,
an old-school homeless street musician from NYC.
Jane taps her way back slowly to Fritz.)**

Blind Jane:
Are you free enough, yet?
Are you free of your memory sickness?
Are you free to live each room of your life
backwards?

Chorus:

**(The Chorus is everyone but Marlene / Mabuse / Blind
Jane and Fritz)**
Here is not the story of a true star.

Blind Jane:
Is this act hesitant, virginal, bestial, or merely
Instrumental, but with real teeth, too?
Does this act defend or defile the faith?
Does this act live inside a raw, wet skin?
Cleaving and burning?
Bringing it though?

Chorus:
Here is not the hyperspace of a new social ontology.

Blind Jane:
We play, become words, we speak.
Looks like you lost it all again in the ghosting.

Chorus:
Here I lurch and leave the movie.
But a switch inside stays on.

**(Now Mabuse, restored suddenly to full force, speaks as Dr.
Goebbels. Was this always Mabuse masquerading as Blind
Jane? If so, what a jokester! If not, how are we to believe
this tectonic shift? The actor's task, here, is more
Promethean than protean, no?)**

Mabuse / Marlene:
It was the ending we didn't like.
**(Laughs: like something cold and insubstantial
"issuing forth" from a dark cave.)**
A picture such as this must have another ending.
But don't think so hard about it.
(Pause.)

57

You, Yes, YOU! Are the man
Who will give us the big Nazi pictures.

(Mabuse / Marlene holds Fritz's chin
and stares deeply into his eyes.
Is he about to pounce?)

(Mabuse / Marlene drops Fritz's chin like a blighted
potato. M / M morphs into a slow turning drift of
presence around the floor. His / her cane becomes more
like a substantial, potentially lethal appendage than a
prop.)

Mabuse / Marlene:
See you back in the City of Smoke, Fritz.
Crackers and nanners, crackers and nanners.

(M / M moves like slow, viscous fluid (think crude oil spill)
around the space, sounding and testing the geography with
his / her cane / appendage. Perhaps s(h)e's conjured the
City of Smoke; Fritz, don't let that long appendage hook
you into something you don't need to experience.
Didn't you listen to Frank?)

Fritz:
(Down on floor level again. It seems this is where he hears
best, hears most, feels enclosed and comforted by sound.
Don't be lulled, Fritz:
it changes moment to moment.)

His eyes loomed ... like cracked empty kliegs, stealing back
the light, a blurred shift of intention: from head to red
through blue to true, it all froze,
and flickered across his face.

58

Wired to go inside, he was, and to squeeze ... and, listen ...
his feet ... *sensoriet durch die Polizei* ... listen ...*passt auf* ... soft
padded footsteps ... that tune ... that ... Lorre? ... *et tu?* ...
listen ... last night it rained ... *passt auf* ... it rained ... I
dreamed I was naked ... I ...

Chorus:
Fritz? Did you sleep well?
Did your door swing wide?
Was your trance deep enough?
Was the night wind cool against your throat?

Was he waiting for you?
Was he, too, torn in two?
Or finally frozen: within the laws of walls?
Or were you?
Did you finally puncture?
Were you free, then?
Did you ever wonder how?

12. "What s(h)e knows without knowing it that no one else quite does": a lesson in applied Entropy"

(Fritz is drawn to M / M – ultimately, he's hooked by that
dangerous appendage. Oww! They move around the stage
slowly, in synch. They do not touch physically but, psycho-
physically, they are sheltering a fragile fire between their
bodies. Maybe this fire is residue from the City of Smoke.
Maybe it's stolen fire and there will be a future issue of
restitution, or worse yet, retribution. This sheltering will
be nearly their last piece of significant stage business.
Before sleep, or back to the City.)

59

(Josef does the bold face parts, again. We hope this
compensates in some small measure for the indignities and
abuse he endured from Billy Wilder.
Really, Josef, it's the best deal we can offer you.)

Chorus:
It's the last night
Says the actor
The audience grows still and looks toward the silence
Looks toward the protagonistas
The actor focuses attention back on them
With a look

Fritz:
I killed him.
After the Testament of Doktor Mabuse.
I tell you, the sonafabitch is dead for me.

Chorus:
They are exposed again in the intense light
On the brink
In the intense light
Their faces turned toward the audience
The outside, the intense light
Always, already

They seem overwhelmed by the silence

(A Big Pause in sound and motion.
For the Silence.)

(Fritz briefly "breaks contact" with M / M.)

Fritz:
(Casting about in 320 degrees.
He really needs to be heard.

It's like clapping for Tinkerbelle.)

All my life I have lived *durch meine augen*.
You know: we should all have eyes all around our heads.
But now ... between the dim power of my own eyes
And the lens of my camera,
Now when I need light most, I can see nothing ...
Nothing but fog, smoke, shadows and dust.

Chorus:
Their expression is one of fear, distress
Says the Actor
Guilt at having always been the center of attention
Guilt for both the actors on the stage
And guilt, too, for the audience

Fritz:
I am tickled pink ... I say anything ...
What else could I say?
I think only how ... how do I get out of here?

Chorus:
Here is not the story of a true star.

(Marlene / Mabuse swirls – we've seen that move before – and hooks Fritz back into the central orbit of this history. The fragile fire is, however, *kaput*.)

Fritz:
I know my death is no solution.
No matter what they tell you: Death Is No Solution.
Jetzt, der Tod ist müde.

61

Marlene / Mabuse:
(Maybe more intimate than before, maybe it just seems that way because of proximity. This is probably Marlene, though we wouldn't take bets. Signifiers and characters (and what's the difference, really, here?) are perhaps all like wet bars of soap in a shower. Perhaps this whole piece should be played in a shower, but with Goebbels possibly in the mix ... well, I wouldn't trust that savage, murderous bastard no matter how dead he appears to be. With Frank, however, hmm ... that's a luminous prospect.)

One last phrase
Says the actor
May perhaps
Have been spoken
Before silence
Settled in
Like frost

(Marlene / Mabuse removes the Mabuse ½ mask and tosses it to Fritz. He drops it like a hot potato. S(h)e shakes out her hair, stretches, removes all vestiges of Mabuse revealing her iconic costume from - (hint: remember the name of a North African country know for its semi-coerced participation in black-ops "extraordinary renditions," especially during a fairly recent (unfinished) war with all its Byzantine *realpolitik*). She repeats the open position, head thrown back.)

Josef:
DONE

(As Josef announces DONE, Marlene freezes.
All others – save Fritz – walk off.)

(As in prologue: film clips from *Testament*, *Destiny*, *Hangmen* provide the visual substrate for Fritz as he explores Frozen

Marlene. Like swimming through a sea of light and evanescent objects, he moves around her, touches her skin, tentatively – so what do you think, Fritz? Something like alabaster, like marble, like that same hollow laugh from the back recesses of that same spooky cave?)

(After a couple circuits of tentative shuffling, touching, (approach and avoidance), he moves to leave. Then he stops. He moves to leave, again ... stops, moves (but it's more difficult, now), stops ... looks backward at Marlene ... and freezes, too.)

(Slow fade to black.)

REALLY DONE

Dire Moon Cartoons

Big White Chair

PART 1

That Mouse Needs a Woman ... Needs a Man ... Needs a Woman ... Needs a ...

Cast:

The Mouse Van Gogh: s(h)e wears high-gloss roller-girl skater drag with big pockets for the MVG's many goods: the *Helmut of Amnesia*, The *Empty Magic Banana* aka *Dead 'Nanner* and the *Boss Cannoli*.

Voice of the Moon Bird: conjured up by the Mouse Van Gogh.

And the Big Noise aka Nasty Voice: obtrusive, jangly, jarring, sometimes intimidating & crass, and usually off-key.

Set: in-between

Time: extremely urgent

Action: duck & cover alternates with defiant "Song of Myself."

At Rise:

(The Mouse Van Gogh zooms into view on rollerblades or skates.)

(Big Noise: thumps, heavy feet, breaking glass, shouts, whistles, panting & ominous wheezes. The din builds. The Mouse Van Gogh stops abruptly: cringes, cups, covers, ducks & (re)covers.)

(Din stops. Throughout this first routine the Mouse Van Gogh screeches to a halt, speaks, skates again, stops abruptly, and speaks at all times in a jitter, looking behind, in front, up on the ceiling, into the wings, as the Big Noise shatters her / his focus or something internal prompts her / his attention to shift.)

Mouse van Gogh

That Mouse ...

(Mouse Van Gogh skates again ... abruptly stops.)

That Mouse ...

(MVG skates again ... abruptly stops. As MVG attempts to speak, the Big Noise erupts, again. MVG stops, cups, cowers ... and speaks while massaging her / his big polyethylene ears.)

Ouchie-Ouch and Gadzooks! Show some love for these tender ears, my dears!

(MVG rises.)

That Mouse really needs a woman. Or a man. Or a woman.
Or ... WHATEVER!

(Pause. MVG skates and speaks)

Whereas this mouse!

68

(MVG skates and beams: this is like a victory lap.)

Whereas this mouse!!

**(Big Noise erupts at even greater decibels. Interrupted by siren,
then a Nasty Voice that really means it:)**
"OK, Punk. Pull up your bloomers.
Jam it back in your pants.
Show me your hairy palms.
Slow now … reeeaal slooow."

**(MVG crouches and cowers during the Big Noise & Nasty Voice
routine. Then MVG rises slowly
and looks all around and points out & up…)**
Whereas that mouse got's no grip no way.

**(The MVG scopes left & right,
then speaks: front & up,
accelerating toward escape velocity.)**

Hey MOON BIRD:
peel your bootie off the ceiling
cuz' it don't count
it's not his
it's not hers
it's not even mine
not never
so you best get smooth
bite down
chew your own lunch
on your own
Holistically!!

**(The MVG grabs her / his own head like a big headache
and speaks to the audience.)**

Diggit: it's sort of like another cross-wired, nervous night when I
can't no how pry this world of stuff and disappointment – O-the
sadness, O-the deep dismay – off my back and just sleep, You know
really sleep, cuz' you got to know
it's in my genes and my own whole family – it's absolutely part of
my phylum, dontcha' know – to fidgit and to jitter, to galumph –
FORTISSIMO! – back & forth & back & forth & then, finally,
when I almost get the ceiling and the walls and the floor to go
inside
and expand, and confer, and expand
and confer, some more, and ...

**(MVG stops. Does "significant whisper" to audience, looking left
and right, all around as punctuation.)**

... look: this could be the for real horizon of some beau coup true,
revolutionary event.
In a nearly normal galaxy
– **(Aside:** OH YEAH, and where, indeed, would that be) –
– You'd need your own imbedded radar to even hear
the far and the near
the news through these
big, beautiful polyethylene ears
of THIS MOUSE, THIS MOUSE
THIS – MAGNUM – MOUSE

(Pause for applause and the MVG works it.)

... but this here galaxy is the odd duck.
It all starts off, OK
or at least, more evener
then – BAM! – this crazy MOON BIRD
– looking first off like a sweet, sweet angel ...
– BUT, Uh-Uh! –
This Mouse instantaneously scopes

70

clandestine patterns of BIG BOGUS!
like lightening and ... anyway,
this crazy MOON BIRD is stuck to my ceiling
like a cartoon cat.
Then this MOON BIRD says to lil' *moi*:

**(In Voice of Crazy Moon Bird while in italics.
Of course the MVG supplies that voice:)**

"Naked Christian
Naked Jew
Kiss your furry turtle
Make that furry-furry turtle
Operate
Just for you."

Then
The MOON BIRD says again to me:
"da' big boss poke de' sweet
bird angel
dead eye, in both eyes
with a magic jewel
- a Ruby, yet -
and, 'doze formerly avian angelized eyes
are Trans – Mog – Ri - Fied
into scary lasers
that turn enemy and friend, alike
into creepy little skellingtons
of gray ash / smelly bone
quick as grease: so
don't be working on my nerves, so
don't you piss me off"

And so says this sorry crazy MOON BIRD,
for sure no angel,
just a loon

And so says, I:
Craaaazy!!!
It's a Mythic-Mythic moment
It's eerie and it's joy, together.
Better than a month's trial marriage to any member of
any officially recognized species
and thoroughly phenomenal, spiritually risky
like gaz-o-line
like big, dumb, polyethylene
like ...

(Again, the Big Nasty Voice erupts:)
No Dice. No Dice. You Mice Know Too Much.

**(MVG cups, cowers and scopes again. Then recovers.
Then juts her / his chin and speaks.)**

Hey, MOON BIRD
You a facile jerk?
Or just a cal-cu-lat-ed goof?
Huh? Rarely?
Hardly Ever?
Seldom Seen?
Sometimes?
Almost Never?
Or Really: Never – Never - Never?

(MVG speaks to the audience.)

Less than never even, Jeez!
I'm stuck.
How's a Mouse ever gonna'
Embody & Ensoul what's actual
with this kinda' lousy shout
ping-pongin' in my brain pan?

(Big Pause.)

Well, Lookitdis!!

**(The MVG rummages in one
of her / his big pockets.)**

If I can just get this ... this ... this ...
Yeah, this ...

(MVG brandishes the Helmut of Amnesia.)

... Helmut of Amnesia workin' for me ...

**(The MVG tries to jam the Helmut of Amnesia
on her/ his head. It won't go over
her/ his big dumb polyethylene ears.
The MVG tosses off the Helmut of Amnesia.)**

Hell's Bell's!

(Pause.)

If I could work up a decent case of amnesia ... if I could
even find a beach before the bomb or the black mayonnaise
or the death-kit hits...
But ...

**(The MVG pulls out The Mostly Empty Magic Banana
aka Dead 'Nanner from another pocket.)**

Aha! I still got my dead 'nanner.

**(MVG offers this "object of deepest reverence"
to the audience as a big boon.)**

73

Can't ever go wrong with a 'nanner.

**(Now the Mouse Van Gogh drops the 'nanner
and pulls out the Ultimate Boss Canoli.)**

Or, and especially, the Ultimate Boss Cannoli!

**(The MVG nibbles, sucks and licks
the Ultimate Boss Cannoli, and then speaks.)**

... Now 'dis ... is some kinda ...
insane traaaans – portation.

**(The Mouse Van Gogh speaks from somewhere
in her / his own inner hyper-space.)**

Alas / Alas
Annette flunks her
Apgar test... Yet again

**(Then, Bam! The MVG is back again
from inside into out.)**

Whew! That one almost did me,
Between a blur and a purr.
Between a mega-ton cum
and the Ultimate Boss Cannoli:
ain't no doubt and
ain't no contest.

(The MVG "tests the air" with ears and tongue.)

So I guess it's time for me to do the beach
and get more intimate
with my own ... furry turtle.

**(Another nibble-suck-lick bite.
Another act of insane transportation.)**

Yessireedee!!
Most indubitably!!
This is how a world starts ... for Reals!

**(The Mouse Van Gogh wanders
over to the Big White Chair
in a sweet Boss Cannoli daze.)**

PART 2

Big White Chair

Cast:

The Mouse Van Gogh (MVG) / "Zack": central character, intrepid rodent, incorrigible romantic, gifted with insight and techie-powers: a true hero, MVG also doubles as "Zack": the most powerful and malignant member of the *3-Z Brothers Political & Economic Extortion Cartel. Zack is the Brainiac of the 3-Zs*, but no match for the exuberantly joyful intellect of the Mouse Van Gogh. Script indicates where MVG transforms into "Zack," and where that transformation reverses. When Mouse Van Gogh plays Zack, that name is always in quotation marks: i.e. "Zack".

Zed: "brother" of Zack & Zucheo. A lesser god. Since the dubious "disappearance" of Brother Zack, they are now known as *3-Z Brothers (minus) 1. Zed is often described as the Conniving Core of the 3-Zs*, and may be considered the de facto group leader in Zack's absence.

Zucheo: "brother" of Zack & Zed. Lesser, yet, even. *The Big Muscle – certainly not the brains – of the 3-Z Cartel.* Most useful for evictions, erasures, and to clean up the ensuing mess when things get physical. Even Mama couldn't love poor Zucheo, and he carries that baggage. Sad.

Note: Even though the 3-Zs are described as brothers, they could also be sisters, cousins, or even unrelated, genetically. Most importantly: *These characters are not gender-specific.* For example, one obvious possible configuration might be: Mouse Van Gogh/ "Zack" (female), and Zed - Zucheo as males.

Props / Sight Gags:

The Big White Chair, Big Dumb Polyethylene Ears/Flexible Head Fins, Used Cheroot, (Possibly) Bootleg 3rd Eye Implant, Boot of Contention, Flower (and Vase), the Magic Sandwich, Monster Pliers, Giant Clothespin, Auld Alarum Clock and Nifty Keel-Hawler Jammies are all props conceived as larger-than-life Sight Gags. They have no preconceived template freeing up the producing theatre's design team's creative energies to go as minimal / maximal as desired. Many of these props were inspired by children's toys.

The Funky Screen may be embedded in wall or positioned / suspended anywhere else so that it's visible for both actors and audience without interrupting sight lines. Various slides serve as *Thought / Image Balloon Sight Gags* **that often contradict or clarify implications of the dialogue.**

Tech:

The only tech involved in *Big White Chair* – beyond construction of the Prop / Sight Gags – is occasional projection of slides that serve as commentary on plot / dialogue or as stand-alone images. These slides, commensurate with the broad-stroke cartoonish plot, characterization and thematic thrust of the play, are currently all completed and available upon request. A new set of slides could be designed for the production in-house - if producing company so desires. The *Big White Chair* should be construed as somewhat of a throne – in keeping with it's cachet as a power object in the play, and with its mundane function as a toilet in the real world.

Style:

The dialogue in *Big White Chair* often scans as poetry – thus the configuration of the line breaks. The pace, rhythm and formatting of the dialogue was intended to emphasize sound values, and also as aids to memorization, phrasing / accenting for the actors. The visual frame and broad-stroke, exaggerated action styling derives from *Commedia Dell'Arte* to a certain extent, but also from the silent movie era work of *Mack Sennett* and *Charlie Chaplin*. In many ways,

the Z Brothers could be characterized as an evil incarnation of the
Keystone Cops.

Big White Chair

At Rise:

(Mouse Van Gogh mounts the *Big White Chair* – a porcelain
commode – as if preparing to crank out an alimentary sonata.
MVG's other stuff surrounds *Chair: Used Cheroot, (Possibly) Bootleg
3rd Eye Implant, Boot of Contention,* the *Flower (in Vase), The Magic
Sandwich, the Auld Alarum Clock.* The *Funky Screen* is visible for
audience and actors. MVG surveys domain, reads paper,
sitting / smoking Cheroot.)

Mouse Van Gogh (speaks/sings:)
Chubby-chubby in a big ol' boojam tree, my right arm, tight across
my angel
like a sweet, 3-note song ...
**(The Mouse Van Gogh grunts and strains on Chair.
MVG's Angel appears on screen.)**
... oh yeah, no science, no philosophy, no blame
... like a lie talkin' back ...
(MVG gazes at Angel and sighs.)
... inside your brain it all begins ...
(MVG jumps off Chair, hits stage, does up bloomers and sings:)
... where your own feet are ...
(The MVG stubs out Cheroot in Flower Vase.)
... right here, right there ...
... right now, my Angel says *Wake UP*!
(Auld Alarum Clock rings!)
And jitter onna' razor! Oww!
This fine new day inside my fine new eye
of Babylon. And that's my own eye, too.

(The Mouse Van Gogh installs Third Eye Implant in forehead.
It glows Pan-Optical Illusory.)

Pan-optical!! Illusory!! So cool, so cool!
If you know just how to dial up *da' power*.

(MVG blows kiss toward Screen.
Sweet Angel disappears.)

Now: I must patrol this Zone of Unlove.
All these perimeters ... you know ... got some worry,
got some flex. I must patrol and patrol.
No attachment to outcomes. 'Til the buzz and the tickle
and the bomb comes down. Flex that flux, uh-huh!
Oooh, it's all so damn feelable!

(The MVG checks stuff: sniffs Boot, licks Flower, inspects Magic
Sandwich, runs finger over seat of Big White Chair. MVG paces in
"patrol mode" – a wired state of bluff, tension and alertness. MVG
shows and talks while on patrol in the Zone.)

(Slides: the Honduran and Blue Monks flash on
when MVG refers to them.)

From these bricks all the way to where those hooks stick out: all
that stuff belongs to ... *The Honduran*.
(Pause.) He's tricky. He's fast.
The Honduran steady pushes. Yessireedee,
all these perimeters got some worry, got some flex.
(MVG whirls and jabs finger in opposite direction.)
And over there: the border of the Realm of *The Blue Monks*.
If death enters from that direction, Hah!
Kiss your chronology goodbye, buster! All this light you love must
crack! (Pause.) For now ... the flank holds.
But I can feel it stir, I can feel it worry.

79

I can taste the flux on my tongue.

(The MVG probes the air with quivering tongue.)

O-me-o-my, how them dice do dance 'til the ol' potato gets too hot to hold ... or juggle, even.

- BUT Wait A Minute: Who Are These Bad Oscars? —

(Zed and Zucheo enter from opposite sides. They wear identical black hats / black cowboy dusters. They do *Dance of the 3-Z Brothers Minus 1* and meet up center stage. Then they move around stage in manic bursts; take turns "on point" while other covers. As soon as MVG sees them, MVG aims body straight at them – resolutely – through *3rd Eye Implant*. Eventually, Zed & Zucheo pin MVG.)

>   **Zucheo**
>   Ok, Freeze!

>   **Zed**
>   Get down! Right here!

>   **Zucheo**
>   Don't move your head!

>   **Zed**
>   Don't talk ... to anyone!

>   **Zucheo**
>   I said: FREEZE!

>   **Zed**
>   And I'll just confiscate this Third Eye.
>   **(Zed grabs the MVG's Third Eye Implant
>   & installs it on his own forehead.)** Cute little gizmo.

**(Zed activates the Third Eye Implant.
But: he doesn't know the code to dial it up, safely.)**
Huh!!!
**(Zed stumbles to his knees, flails about, moans and
desperately deactivates the Third Eye Implant.)**
Nothing but blur. Nothing but blur.
Must be a bootleg. **(Zed queries the MVG.)**
How much did you pay for this model?

Zucheo
I said: don't talk to anyone.

Mouse Van Gogh
Oh Shit, Angel!
I think the Monks have broken / through the border.
(Zucheo whacks the MVG with his hat at the /.)

Zed
Don't talk. Don't turn your head.

Zucheo
So, do I smoke the Mouse? Eat it up? Or piss on it?

Zed
Hard choice.
But I'm sure this Mouse knows something.

Zucheo
Cool! We interrogate him.

**(Zed & Zucheo produce *Monster Pliers*.
One grabs the MVG's tail, the other MVG's nose with pliers.
They lead MVG over to *Chair* and sit him down.)**

Zed
Sit down. Straight back. Breathe short: Staccato.

81

Now: Ostinato. Now: Pizzicato.
(Pause.) Arco on the down-low, Mouse.

Zucheo
Don't move your head. Don't talk to anyone.

Zed
Except us.

Zucheo
When we say shit, Mouse, you best grunt and produce.

**(Zed & Zucheo pace around MVG, hands behind backs. They stop,
bow up, glare, then pace some more.)**

Zed
You don't recognize us? Do you?

Zucheo
Our Re-Cogni ... Our Re-Cognizerab ... Our Re-Cernazab ...

Zed
That's a hard word, Zucheo. Take your time, Bruddah.

Zucheo
(After he takes a big, deep noisy breath, he blurts it out.)
Our Re-Cog-Niz-A-Bility Quotient is
Way toned. Way down.

Zed
Two tone, one tone, no tone about it.

Zucheo
(With a Big Whisper:)
Really, We're into deep cover. High Drag.
We're In-Cog-Ni-To!

82

Zed
But we're Zed

Zucheo
And Zucheo

Zed & Zucheo (Together.)
We're the Rulers of Our World!!

**(The MVG jabs finger in direction
of Screen. Slide: Zed, Zack & Zucheo together:
Zed & Zucheo are choking Zack.)**

Mouse Van Gogh
Oh Yeah. **(Big Yawn.)**
I know how that goes:
(MVG sings a sort of hip-hop 3-Z jingle.)
Zack, Zed & Zucheo are the Rulers of Our World
Say Zack say Smoke, Say "Stir it up," Say Zed say Shoot,
Say Zucheo, Say ... Say ...Say: Zuk, Zuk, Zuk.
**(Zucheo makes Zuk, Zuk, Zuk
like "tommy-gun" with sync with MVG.)**

Zucheo
You got that one down. Mouse.

Zed
Embodied, we are. Before you, we be.

Mouse Van Gogh
The Rulers of our World, Huh?

Zucheo
What you say, Mouse! What you see!

Mouse Van Gogh
I say: smoke it! I say: stir it up!
Go on, make it worry! Make it jump: chumps!

(Chumps that they be, Zed & Zucheo
just can't make it jump. See?)

(Slide: Zack face down with a knife in his back.)

(Zed & Zucheo do a double-take with deep unease
at sight of image on funky screen.)

Mouse Van Gogh
See? If you two rule the world, you got a gap: Zed, Zucheo, used to
be 3. So where's Zack?

Zucheo
That's a ... a question.

Zed
Not so fast. You are authorized to metabolize.
Only that. We ask all the questions.

(The MVG points to the Funky Screen again.
Slide: Zack's head lopped off by guillotine.)

(Zed & Zucheo feel the heat of impending
retribution and double-take, again.)

Zucheo
Uh ... uh ... Zack checks up on all our stuff.

Zed
You got that right. Zack's the Lord of Long Range Operations.
He's on his way to Tierra del Fuego ...
... as we speak.

Zucheo
We got lots of stuff. Even there!

Zed & Zucheo
Have we got stuff? Say, have we got stuff?
We got stuff everywhere!

Zed
Here now, too. Plant the 3-Z **(aside:)** *minus 1* – Flag, Zucheo.
We're here to pacify and eat.
We have nothing to explain.
(Zucheo plants the 3-Z minus 1 flag.
One Z is Xed over.)
You see, we're organized.

Zucheo
We know how and when to move.

Zed
It's all part of: *Extreme SYNCHRONETICS!*
High-End conceptual activity, But *embodied,* too.
Awesome is much too tame a word!

Mouse Van Gogh
So what's the real deal, Cuz?
And where does this deal go down?

Zed
The deal is the ground whereon you sit.

Zucheo
We like the weather here. We like the view.
The only hitch: **IS YOU!**

Zed
(To Zucheo.) And that's your cue.
**(Zucheo tries to pry the Mouse Van Gogh off
Chair. MVG resists and they shove back & forth.)**

Mouse Van Gogh
Whoa there, Tex!
You don't know the layout. You can't use this stuff, yet.
And what about the Honduran? The Blue Monks, too?

Zucheo
Fee – Fie – Fooey on the Honduran.
(Pause.)
The Honduran is less than ca-ca.   I light him up and piss him out,
and let the wind blow him gone away.

Zed
Then we buy the Blue Monks. They've been bought before.

Mouse Van Gogh
And the Big White Chair I sit upon?
You don't know how to operate this chair, now.
Do you?

Zed
Point well made: Brother, apply some leverage.
Make our Mouse sing!

**(Zucheo grabs the Mouse Van Gogh's big dumb
polyethylene ear with his Monster Pliers.)**

Zucheo
Say what, Mouse? Say what?

Mouse Van Gogh
OOWW, I say!! Let go, Jim!

I'll tell you what you want to hear.
Just turn loose my ear.

Zucheo
HoKay! We say shoot, you shoot, M-M-Mouse.

Mouse Van Gogh
Tokay! And yesterday, I sit upon my Big White Chair.
And I see a cloud. With shoulders.

Zed
You don't say?

Mouse Van Gogh
But I do. A pink cloud. With shoulders.
With flex. With substance. Feelable, too.
You know what I'm saying?
Sometimes, the whole thing breathes like a person.
But it's not.

Zucheo
Bor-ing.
**(Zucheo latches Monster Pliers back on MVG's ear.
But he waits before he cranks down.)**
Tell me something I can use
or bite down on the wrath of Zucheo!

Zed
(To Zucheo, who backs off in a funk.)
Chill, Zucheo. Turn off that lizard in your brain.
(To the MVG, as crafty Zed leans closer.)
Tell me more about this chair. You turn it on, where?

Mouse Van Gogh
(Demos while he talks.)
You sit like so. You face front.

87

You strain to make what you need. You grunt ...
(MVG grunts) ... and your desire appears.
(Zed looks down and around the Chair.
MVG points to the Funky Screen.)
No. Up there.

(Slide: MVG's Sweet Angel fills screen
as Foxy Apparition.)

(MVG puts his arm around Zed's shoulder.)
Sometimes, I sit upon this chair all night.
I chew the fog and wait, and Sweet Angel appears.
Sometimes, my Angel's lips talk right inside my ear.
(Very loud, the MVG, now: right in Zed's ear.)
O-My-Angel!! **(Pause.)** Sometimes, from this very spot, There's no
other there, but here. Right here. This Chair. *Dialed & Gone!*
Uh-Huh, Da-Dee-O!
(Pause.) Pretty cool, you would agree?

Zed
The devil's own toothpick!
I gotta' get this Chair to work for me.
(Zed picks up Magic Sandwich, sniffs, opens it,
and licks the insides: WOW!)
This sandwich, too! I *WANT* this sandwich!

Mouse Van Gogh
Not a problem. Just supply the bread.
The rest is there when you dismount the Big White Chair.
It's residue.
(MVG calls Zed closer, looks over at Zucheo,
says to Zed in a Big Whisper.)
A secret process of the chair.

Zed
Oh this Dig is too damn hot!

88

I gotta' jump on that Chair! Gotta' Munch & Chew!
Brew me up an image of: *My Own Heart's Desire*.
(Zed to MVG.)
A deal's a deal, Mouse. You can vacate right now.
**(Zed whips MVG off Big White Chair. MVG lands on feet.
Zed occupies the Chair.)**

Mouse Van Gogh
So: what's it worth? What's the damage?
What'll you give me for it?

Zed
Give you? **(Zed laughs.)** Give you?
**(Zed summons Zucheo out of his deep funk.
Holds up MVG's boot.)** We'll just give you the boot.

Mouse Van Gogh
No Deal. What good's one boot?
(Pause.) Besides. And formerly, that boot was mine, already.

Zed
(Zed takes dainty bite of the Magic Sandwich.)
O-Mouse, I think you got the point.
And O-I-Truly-Dig ... this sandwich.

(Zucheo grabs MVG for "Old Heave-Ho".)

Zucheo
Time to fly O-Mousie-Mouse. Here comes Kitty-Kitty.

Mouse Van Gogh
Wait, wait, you gotta' wait! This acquisition is serious.
You can't move a situation this complex without Zack.
Only he knows how to read the flex and redirect the flow.

Zed

Tierra del Fuego is a long ways off, Mouse. We can't wait.
Synchronetics Won't Wait!

Zucheo

We got Zack's powerful attorney Pow! Pow!
In advance of the big dance!

Zed

Right Zuk.
But too much information, Bruddah.
(Zed says to MVG.)
Each contingency is considered and covered whilst Zack is
incommunicado.
As we speak, he strokes like a sleek torpedo
toward the rocky coast of Tierra del Fuego.

Zucheo

That's right. Last time I saw Zack, he was in the water.

**(Slide: Zack sinks to bottom wearing
pair of "Cement Booties.")**

(Zed & Zucheo scope slide, double-take, yet again.)

Zed

Zack said: Strike, Seize. Savor the Juice!
He said: twist it off in the interim! 'Til he returns from the bottom
... of the world, that is. And this is all, already, a fait accompli.
Synchronetics as the Iron-Arm of public policy.

**(Slide: Zack's black-hat-wearing skeleton
on the bottom of the sea.)**

**(Zed & Zucheo: another scope, double-take,
and way more deep unease.)**

90

Zucheo
Good ol' Zack. A veritable Back-A-Ruda of Doom.

Zed
OK, Mouse. Fair's fair.
Say, uh ... I give you back this boot?

Zucheo
Yeah! Say it: I give you back this boot.

Mouse Van Gogh
That's MY boot!

Zucheo
Go on and SAY IT: I-Give-You-Back-This-Boot.

Zed
Loose the boot, Zuk. Then Lose this Lousy Mouse.

Zucheo
Oh Yeah! Some Hella' Recreation!

(Zucheo wings boot at MVG.)

Zed
(Zed flips MVG a quarter.)
This seals the deal: 2 bits for a 2-bit rodent. We have no more need
of you. Now be gone. I've got a date with a pink cloud. And you
make my eyes ache, Mouse.

(Zucheo roars something gutteral and weird at MVG.)

(The MVG retrieves quarter, flings it back at Zed.)

Mouse Van Gogh
Your cash ain't nothin' but trash.
Your cash ain't nothin' but trash.
Zap you, Zed! Zap you, too, Zucheo!

**(Zed & Zucheo *Freeze* while the MVG produces the following
ominous vocal stylings:)**

Just dream on, Zed, just dream on, Zucheo
just dream on, all these borders got some flex
you know, got some worry, so just
dream on, 'til you can't bear the Chair

you know, ya'all got's to sleep sometime, somewhere
and the Mouse Van Gogh is right here
right there, never far enough away

**(MVG disappears for a spell.
Zed & Zucheo come back from where they've been.
Zucheo kicks the boot.)**

Zucheo
That Mouse gives me the creeps.
**(Zucheo picks up the flower, sniffs it, sneezes,
throws it down and stomps on it.)**
I Hate that Flower. Who needs a Flower ... like that one?

Zed
Not us, to be sure. Now dial down the decibels.
I'm gonna' use my Chair.

Zucheo
Our Chair! Our Chair!

Zed
Uh ... Right!

92

(Zed faces front. And he strains and he grunts.)
Slide: Zucheo hanged. A decree – "for murder
of Zack" – around his neck.)

(Zucheo scopes the slide, double-takes, and moves on Zed.
Zed is too busy with "His Chair" to care.)

Zucheo
(Pointing at screen.) So what's this? What's this mean? Huh Zed!
Talk to me, Bruddah!

Zed
(Too far gone to see Bruddah Zucheo's POV.)
Why that..that's my pink cloud..with shoulders..that's...

Zucheo
That's Bogus! That's not ...
(Zucheo grabs Zed's throat, tries
to wrestle him from Chair.)
Mama always said you'd float to the top ... like scum.

("Zack" appears. MVG ears stick out from under black hat.
"Zack" wears a black duster like others.)

"Zack"
Well, one-cow-to-another: Where's the cream, Gene?

(Zed & Zucheo jump to attention, bodies rigid
with unease, heads / eyes staring forward.)

Zed & Zucheo
Zack-O-Zack ... you're ... Back?

"Zack"
Em-Bodied.

("Zack" inspects Zed & Zucheo. He adjusts their chins, tweaks
their cheeks, ties Zucheo's shoelaces together
with giant clothespin.
He turns away, then spins back, abruptly, to stare them down.)
Before you: *In-My-Entirety.*

**(Zed & Zucheo huddle as Zack inspects Flower, licks Magic
Sandwich, walks to Big White Chair.)**

Zed
(To Zucheo.) I thought **You** did the deed?

Zucheo
I thought **WE** did it too. But Mama always says inside Zack's brain
... lurks a monster.

Zed
An' Mama don't, Mama don't, Mama don't lie.

Zucheo
You wish.
(Zucheo tries to walk and trips.)
F-F-F-F ... Frack you, Zack!

"Zack"
(Points to Big White Chair.) What's that?

Zed
That's MY...

Zucheo
Our Chair! Our Chair!

"Zack"
(Lifts up lid of Big White Chair and points inside.)
And that?

94

Zed
Merely residue of the previous owner.

Zucheo
He left in a huff, in a big ol' hurry.

("Zack" hops onto the Chair, strains & grunts.)

(Slide: Zed & Zucheo, facedown, knives in backs.)

Zed & Zucheo
Hey! What's the deal here? Talk to us, Zack!

"Zack"
("Zack" looks up at Slide.)
A silly little glitch. And merely.
A wrinkle in the nap of the galactic flow.
(Zacks hops down from the Big White Chair.)
Did ya' miss me, Bruddahs?

Zed
(Bows deep to honor Zack.)
Sin of my skin.

"Zack"
No blame like a lie talkin' back at me.
(To Zucheo.) And what about you, Sir Muttonhead?

Zucheo
I-Miss-You-Very-Much. Zack. Bruddah, Zack.

"Zack"
A solid lie, it talks again.
(Pause.) So what's the fresh attraction? The new dig?
The layout and environs? All the new stuff, and shit?

Zucheo
(Points to the Chair.)
A repo, and merely. This Mouse couldn't come up with the juice.
So we stiffed him!

Zed
We did it in remembrance of **YOU**, Zack!

Zucheo
Bruddah!

"Zack"
Easy backbrain lowrent kinda' lie.
(Big Whisper to audience.) You just gotta' love it.
(To Zed & Zucheo.)
Every time I go to check on our stuff in Fuego, You guys develop
some new way to Spend **MY** Money! And I won't forget the little
swim. Just like a health club, indeed!
**(Zucheo follows behind "Zack",
mimes narration of the "little swim".)**
Goddamn pirates!
Cyber-octopi ... The Sargasso Surprise ...... Unspeakable Filth ...
Nuclear Doom ...Boom-Boom-Boom all night in the Hoarse
Latitudes. If it weren't for my flexible head fins,
("Zack" waggles big dumb polyethylene ears.)
and my nifty keel-hawler jammies,
("Zack" flashes jammies under his black duster.)
I woulda' been crabmeat. A bunch of times.
("Zack" spins abruptly, catches Zucheo's routine.)
Zuk, hit your stash.
Did you forget or forego your Ritalin, again?
(To Zed.) And don't tell me you didn't know about the possibility

96

of trauma to the solitary swimmer.

Zed
I only know that you enjoy a challenge.

"Zack"
Yeah? Well I hereby challenge you to buy me
breakfast, lunch and dinner, all at once.
Abolish Chronology, Hells Bells, I could eat
A bear, a bug, or a bird, broasted or toasted,
sauteed or raw, your arm ... or ... or his leg ...
("Zack" leaps for Zucheo's leg & chomps.)

Zucheo
(Hopping around with "Zack" attached to his leg.)
Yowwweee!

(Zed & Zucheo quick throw money together.
"Zack" turns loose Zucheo's leg.)

Zed & Zucheo
(Zed & Zucheo toss coins & bills toward Zack.)
Here! Chow down! Do what you need to do!

"Zack"
("Zack" gathers up his swag.)
And when I get back I'll need some down time on that Chair.
You Dig?

Zed
Precisely!

Zucheco
No sweat, Zack. Just jet!

97

"Zack"
CIAO-CIAO-CIAO!
I'll cop a loaf of bread, too.
Don't want to run out of ... Magic Sandwiches.
(Pause. "Zack" picks up the 3rd Eye Implant.)
I sure hope you didn't screw around with this
"BOOTLEG" 3rd Eye Implant.
If you did, it's curtains, Bruddahs.
Nothing left but a big bad blur, forever.
The carnage in your lobe is ... *irreversible.*

**(Zed massages former site of his "BOOTLEG" 3rd Eye Implant
on forehead, and moans. Zucheo snickers.)**

**("Zack" strolls off, loses hat and cowboy duster,
reinstalls 3rd Eye Implant. Now, the <u>Mouse Van Gogh rides again</u>,
winks at audience in Big Whisper.)**

Mouse Van Gogh
Unless you got the knack. Unless you know the codes.

(The *Implant* lights up all MVG's essential chakras.)
... Ahhh!!! My little Shantih Blossom. I'm back home again.
**(After a series of pick & roll-ish fakes on one other, Zed & Zucheo
race for the Big White Chair. Of course, Zed gets there first.
Again.)**

Zed
**(Sitting on Big White Chair, rubbing his empty Third Eye socket.
Zed strains and grunts in synch with the Chair,
and fends off fuming Zucheo.)**
Lay off, Bruddah, go visit Mama. I got to chew some fog
whilst' I still can do it.

**(They wrangle, while Mouse Van Gogh sits on the edge of the stage
and Big Whispers to the audience.)**

(The Mouse Van Gogh sings MVG's Dream Time Song.)

Mouse Van Gogh
Now, Hee-Hee-Hee!
Watch the complications ensue.
Cuz' they gotta' share the Chair.
Hey youse, hey flex, hey wear it out,
O-Thou 3-Z Rulers of Our World (Minus 1).

**(Slide: Zack & Zucheo carry Zed on their shoulders
on a golden litter.
Zed sits on *Chair* with crown.)**

Zucheo
(Zucheo points to *Funky Screen* as he speaks.)
Hey! What's this? Talk to me, Zed! Bruddah!
**(Zed ignores Zucheo, and strains and grunts.
Zucheo scans the horizon. Searching for Zack.)**
Mama always said ...F-F-F-F ... Frack you, Zack.

Zed
(While he strains and grunts on Big White Chair.)
And Mama don't Mama don't Mama don't lie.

**(Zucheo grabs Zed's throat to throttle and choke him.
They struggle, they struggle, they struggle ... they FREEZE.)**

Mouse Van Gogh
(To audience.)
Then again, maybe it just don't wear out, not never.
Maybe it's feelable *ad infinitum.* Maybe some flux, maybe some flex,
but maybe never worry, anymore. So, maybe now: The Mouse Van
Gogh says: it's Dreamtime, once again.

**(Slide: Mouse Van Gogh's Sweet Angel reappears on screen
in full psychic combat mode.)**

(The Mouse Van Gogh sings MVG's Dream Time Song.)

My Angel, O-my Angel, no philosophy but sky-
skin for all us sky people, there it is, again,
with no need to be, just that buzz, again,
that sweet electricity: wet wide mouth, red lips inside my ear,
my love bomb, O-my Angel, my bullet of bliss,
my sweet, 3-note song.

DONE

PART 3

Stroker Del Fuego

Cast:

Zack: (aka The Mouse Van Gogh, at some point)

Zed & Zucheo: The *3-Z Rulers of Our World (Minus 1)*

The **Stroker Del Fuego** is a *Sargasso Class Rave Digga'* vessel of opportunity (aka Privateer). The Stroker's hull, deck, etc. is composed of the **Big White Chair** and a long, wide plank set on milk crates or something equally simple. The plank serves as seating for galley slaves (i.e. Zed & Zucheo), and as a bridge for Captain Zack. It also retains its traditional role in schemes of Justice, pirate style.

Props & Situation Notes:

The form of the **Awesome Insignia of Thrust** should be commensurate with its function.
Zed's **Mic** may be toy or real, but must accentuate the eerie timbre of Zack's voice, post (possible) **Implant** malfunction.
The **Mighty Hammer of Zucheo** is a hefty pig, indeed.
Zed's diagnosis of Zack's meltdown from use of **BOOTLEG Third Eye Implant** is problematic. Equally problematic is Zed's prognosis for Zack (MVG)s bleak future.
The **Magic Sandwich Bread** is pliable enough to hide in Zack (MVG)'s bloomers.
The **Mythic Pristine Sistine Finger** could be composed as a "human sculpture" by Zed and Zucheo. Or it could be another apparition, say an actual Pristine Sistine, directly, on the Funky Screen.

101

At Rise:

(Slide: Del Fuego Dome of Simultaneous
Multi-Joy Channel Stimulation.)

Zack
Del Fuego, O Del Fuego: rub it, sweat, rub it yet some more ...
OH YEAH!
(Big Roar.)
alla' proximate surfaces in
beautiful Del Fuego
are Soooo Hot!
**(Captain Zack addresses & exhorts his crew
to stroke more, to stroke harder.)**
Flex and moan and tropostaticize it, Bruddahs.
Into the Zone of Spooky Action
into and through the distant Zone
of There Be Dragons
and flagons of crappy grog.
Jump and cut and bounce it
home again.
Del Fuego, O Del Fuego
we have so much more to share
so much more to learn about each other
and so little time to do to do to do.

Zed
Easy said for you, Zack.
Up there steering us.
Your own butt on OUR Big White Chair.

Zucheo
(Zucheo begins to blubber.)
Brud-dah-dah-dah, my own butts hurts.
My back, too.

102

I ain't merely no machine.

Zack
It's hard, it's true.
But it's good for you to stretch your neck out.
Do it for your Captain,
For Mama too.
Work through the pain and build: your own
Magic Sandwich.
New Vistas. Parataxis.
Broad, Multi-Global Points-of-View,
and shit.

**(Zucheo Razzes back at Zack.
Zack bonks him with the MVG's boot.)**

Zed
(Who also blubbers.)
My back & brain are all tweaked, too.
Listen!
My Inner Monster screams; Zack!
Ima' gonna' throttle, choke & stretch
your own neck
hella' long & hella' tight.
You know you got to sleep sometime.
You know you can't stay up all night.

Zed & Zucheo
We hurt bad, Bruddah-Captain.
Much too much of nothing good goin' on.
We demand to be adjusted before we go insane.
All this stroking, all this sweat we suffer
Gets us nothing but
a big pain in our own asses
and a Dead Zone in our brains.
So why do we do all the work for you,

103

And you get all the gains?

Zack
Adjusted? You want to get adjusted?
Hey, you asked and now
you're gonna' get your own souls right.
Look at me, Bruddahs.
I'm stirring up the aethers, just for you.
**(Zack stirs up the aethers like an ancient magician.
Zed & Zucheo show that they feel every nuance.)**
I'm a-stirrin'. I'm a-stirrin'.
Here's comes the big turn
Of the big ol' cosmic screw
in de' nut-sack chakra.
Say: Bestir me' buffos
Say: hot-so, like you mean it
Shimmer-shimmer, say:
I got you pinned inside my populuxe radar,
Once again,
You feel the juice in the adjustment?
So what you say, Bruddahs?

Zed & Zucheo
We say: turn it off, Captain,
Bruddah Zack.
We say: OOOWWWW!

Zack
So Zucheo, me' baddest Bucc-oh,
show a fella' just a little bruddah-love.
and jam this mighty hammer up your left nostril.
With all due haste.

**(Zacks flips the Giant Hammer down to Zucheo
with a little Bruddah-Love ceremony.)**

(Zucheo tries to jam the Giant Hammer up his nose.
Zed stops him. Zed resists every time Zucheo tries
to jam the Giant Hammer.)

Zed
Don't you dare.
Zack, I hope you're with them
when all them hippos are boiled in their tanks.

Zucheo
(Holding Giant Hammer with both hands.
It follows when he moves his head
like a cobra follows a snake charmer's flute.)
Big noise ... insane ... my head ... like a hurricane
Teeth inside my head, Zack ...
Mama always said you were born
With a monster inside your brain.

Zack
Happy haunting, and too,
Inside of you, Bruddah.
And Mama don't Mama don't Mama don't Mama don't lie.

Zed & Zucheo
Hiss you, Mama!

(Zucheo stays stuck to the Giant Hammer.
Sometimes, it comes alive and searches for his nose.)

Zack
(Delivers his elegy, ostensibly for Mama,
but focused more or less on Zack, alone.)
Mama, yes, O Mama.
Indeedy-do, O Mama.
Bestir, bestir it all, just for Mama.
In lieu and honor of the Mama's best Baby-Me.

Of the Buddha
Of True Bamboozlement.
And his Bee-Twang Blue Pompadour.
And his Lust-Button.
And his last Zoom-Beyonding.

**(Captain Zack's moment of silence
in memory of Mama.)**

So back inside the breech, boys.
Strive. Hump. Stroke-Stroke.
C'mon Bruddahs.
Right now, instead trippin' out
You just fakin' the funk.
Again!

Zucheo
Butter my robot, Monkey-Meat.

Zed
I thumb my bum at Thee.

Zack
It is a bitter dose, My Bruddahs,
But you are merely crew.
I didn't say it's fair
It's La Fortuna
it's my tongue says
your sweat equals my money
says, I'm up here
In the Chair.
And you're not.
**(Zack, the Wayfinder, points toward Fuego
with the Awesome Insignia of Thrust.)**
You're down there.
Both of you.

106

Zucheo
You wait!

Zed
Someday!

Zucheo
Our need is big!
Ugly too!

Zed
Our necessity knows no boundary.

Zack
Ho-Hum.
Stroke and pull, boys,
But, sometimes, don't you just wish?
Hey, only I
am high enough evolved
to use the chair and the Third Eye.
Hey, it happens
Only once in de' generation.
**(Zack begins Command Dream Ritual.
Zed & Zucheo lip-synch in a spell.)**

Only I
make manifest, continuous
Synchronetic, simultaneous
Shriek of Appetite,
Multi-grained, Omega-8, Synaptic.
But
also veiled
like every good myth should be
and fundamental, too,
like a blonde fly dancin'

107

on my belly in the sun
(Pause.)
So study hard, Bruddahs,
cuz' fair's fair.
Just do your homework.
Maybe someday you
can buy your own eye, too,
and mount the Chair.

(Zack activates his own Third Eye Implant.)

(Slide: Big Fractal Blast appears on the screen.)

**(Zack's Third Eye Implant appears to be Bootleg.
He snaps, frizzles & fries
while Zed & Zucheo do percussion.)**

Zed & Zucheo
More Voltage, More Voltage, More Voltage we cry!

(Zucheo pokes the "Zack wreckage" with his toe.)

Zucheo
You want some More-O, Juice-O, Monstroso?

Zed
Chill Zuk. I think Zack's finally bought the ol' 4-Day Creeper!
Brain Fusion, Bruddah! Down & Osterized!
(Zed Mics Zack's stream of psycho-babble.)
Speak up, Bruddah. Say us something we can sell.

Zack
**(Like a drooling stooge: crispy-creepy,
thin-eerie babble:)**
Boo-Hoo
Too Much Boo-Hoo,

Skullmates.
Talk-a-talkin' Self-Ways
On the Dream Telephone.
Ribba.
Rubba.
Bubba.
Gump.
Old Black Sun
Before-O?

(Zack hangs slack-lipt', shrunken, shapeless & way-vacant.)

Zed
His cortex is cooked, indeed.

Zucheo
(Knocks on Zack's newly vacant skull.)
No one home today, Bruddah. Or tomorrow, too.
Alla' time, nothing left upstairs but stew.
Wheeeeww!
(Zucheo does Bye-Bye & Frack-You Zack Ritual.)
Bye-Bye, Zack. Bye-Bye. Bruddah.

**(Zed gingerly unscrews the Bootleg Third Eye Implant
from Zack's forehead.
He inspects it thoroughly, carefully, at arm's length so to speak.)**

Zed
His personal Third Eye Implant was Bootleg, too!
**(Then Zed sucks on Zack's Bootleg Third Eye Implant and gets a
jolt of some residual juice.)**
Owww-eee!
If this eye was sippin' rum, instead,
It would to be One-Five-One or more, at least.

Zucheo
Now it's time for Cement Booties &
A Big Swim for Bruddah Zack.

Zed
And the Chair!

Zucheo
And the Chair?

(Zed & Zucheo do a 3-Z (minus 1) ritual hand jive.)

Zed
It's all family, Zuk.
Bonds of blood.
No more locked in senseless struggle.
No More. No More.
We'll make a pact that's fair
And shameless.

**(Zed & Zucheo "do slow mirrors" and talk about it over the Chair
while they fit Zack with Cement Booties.
Sort of a deep Suspicion Ritual.)**

Zed
Sad. Sad. So much frustration, Little Bruddah.
I long to wield the white-heat prod, the iron poker,
the nut-sack cracker.
I ache to scream again and again: More Voltage!!
And make Ol' Zack Spazz Out & Jitter!
But now, Behold the Man:
O-Ecce Homo: I'm afraid he just won't get it.

Zucheo
**(Removes the Awesome Insignia of Thrust
from Zack's limp hands.**

110

He sticks it into his own bloomers.)
You won't need this no more. Neither.
BruD-D-D-D-Dah!

Zed & Zucheo
Now Zack, time for your big swim!

(Zed & Zucheo haul the wreckage of Zack – pliers to nose –
out onto the Pirates' Plank.)

(Zed & Zucheo perform the Solemn
Pre-Execution Prisoners Speech Ritual
with Chest Percussion accompaniment.)

Zucheo
Speak up, Bru-D-D-D-D-Dah!

(Zed reinstalls the Bootleg Third Eye Implant on Zack's forehead,
and dials around for something good.)

Zed
I'll just dial you up some Talkin' Brain to talk through with.
At this point, it won't hurt a bit.
(Zed hits paydirt!)
Rockin'. There you go. Now:
Confess your Crime.
Abjure your position.
Renege Big.
Bruddah!

("Zack" returns. But "changed utterly," and so-so eerie.)

Zack
(From the edge of the Plank.)
This Chair does more than you think.
More than you Remember.

More than you need & More than you wish to bear.
Gay, Straight, Tense, Wigged,
Stoned &/or Transfigured.
Surfin' the Zoom, alla' time.
Has you got the requisite habits of Speed
to Operate?
Has you got the Raw-Bone?
The Hubris?
Has you got the necessary Huevos?

Zucheo
Got-'cher own Rat'chere in my bloomers.
Youse' has been officially stripped.

Zed
Deposed.
Devolutionized.
Dead ... in the water.

Zed & Zucheo
Soooooooooo!
Make it jump, Zack.

**(Zack walks the Plank to "make it jump."
But, suddenly, s(h)e skips back,
blithe spirit that s(h)e is, and sits down in Zucheo's lap
to teach another Bruddahly lesson to his needy Bruddahs.)**

Zack
All this Shitting / shooting / shitting
Ad infinitum.
You know, Bruddah Zed,
and you know it, too, Bruddah Zucheo,
before you shoot your shot
you got's to scope
which end of your Zip or Gat

is really hot,
and which end
merely Loaded.

(Zed & Zucheo Razz & Jeer)

(Then Zack pulls the only extant Magic Sandwich Bread out of his Bloomers. Suddenly, Zed & Zucheo realize their enormous error.)

Zed
O-Awesome!

Zucheo
O-Dialed & Gone!

Zed & Zucheo
Hiss you, Mama!

Zack
And I may be dead, for sure,
but I got all the Bread.
So say Bye-Bye
So say No More
Magic Sandwich.
Henceforth, and irrevocably,
The Chair is Bare.

(Zack tosses his *(possibly) Bootleg Third Eye Implant* like a "Hail Mary Pass" into the waiting hands of Zed & Zucheo. Of course, they scuffle for possession and, of course, Zed strips it from Zucheo's grasp. While Zed reinstalls the *Implant* on his own forehead – here, expectations of rush override Zed's basic instincts for self-preservation - Zack thumbs his bum at Zed & Zucheo, and jumps off the Plank.)

Zed & Zucheo
(Doing Post-Execution Hand & Finger
Jive Ritual while they speak.)
Dead.
Done. Deed.
Dialed & De-lirious!

(Pause. Zed & Zucheo Scope Out & Analyze
each other's moves from across the Chair.)

(The Ol' Push & Shove Ritual Begins. The Ritual veers toward
Harsh Choral riffs with Ominous Harmonics on <u>OUR</u>.)

Zed & Zucheo
OUR Chair
Absolutely!
OUR Chair
Pataphysically!
Our Chair
the Original
Hemisphere of Maximal!
Our Chair!
Say again,
Our Chair!

(Zed & Zucheo Square-Off over their Big White Chair
& Invoke their Hearts' Desires.)

Zucheo
O You Sweet City of Rub & Sweat!
You Winged Piglets,
O You Blue-on-Baby-Blue,
You Balloon-Land.
I'm on my way in a Hurry
in a big Ol' Heat!

114

Zed
All this
Shitting / Shooting / Shitting Biz,
says I needs my Angel Medicine,
Again!

**(Now, from Zed's lips to Zucheo eager ears – and Zed hijacks the
Nuance & Compulsion Tones of Zack in the saying.)**

Zuk, Bruddah.
Show us a little love
With your Mighty Hammer.
In remembrance of me
Do-It-To-It!

Zucheo
**(Zucheo's arm moves slow / instinctual
to Jam the Mighty Hammer up his nose again.)**
Teeth ... Pain ... inside my Brain ...
I can't resist.
(Zucheo Roars and Struggles to resist.)
You can hog The Chair, Zed.
But you can't hide the deed.

Zed
The Ride & the Rush
Is Worth the Breakdown!
**(Zed hops onto the Big White Chair, first,
of course, again, of course, dials up "his" *Third Eye Implant*,
and strains to Make Manifest.)**
Oh, Yeah! Rockin!
**(Slide: Zed / Shiva dances on the head of Zucheo.
Skulls of Zack & Mouse Van Gogh decorate his belt.)**

(Distracted by the Big White Chair, the surge & jolt of the
(possibly) Bootleg Third Eye Implant, and his Chair-Master's Duty,
Zed's mind-lock over Zucheo melts down. Zucheo breaks through,
Shoves and Vies with Zed for his own seat on the Chair. Round &
round they do their hassle-dance, until they freeze.)

(Some parting shots from Bruddah Zack
as s(h)e treads in the waters of coastal Del Fuego.)

Zack
For now,
Forebear, my Bruddahs.
It's back to the chair
again. Back to more like
Ash than Trigger.
More like Teeth
And Wet Fur.
More like the Blah-Blah-Blah-Blah
Talkin' Cure
and still not Magic, enough.
But easy as grease, always in tow,
and sold to the face it fits, you know.
As sure as you will be
The Meat before you will be
the Potatoes, enjoy
your Jones ... Bruddahs ...
before it hacks right into you ...
... before it bites you back.

(Pause. Now, Zack enjoys a Self-Reflective Moment in the surf.)

So now, at the moment,
I'm officially:
Dead, Dialed and Gone.
Just Maybe.
So now, at the moment,

116

I do not no more exist,
Well, Maybe So.
So Now, at the moment,
I do not know whether
I will ever be back, as Zack,
Or not. Or Maybe.
Even if the Implant was just a ploy, indeed,
this constant slap & worry / twitch routine,
this most uneasy head
this *mucho* heavy crown
all this THIS
makes my nerves just itch.

(Pause, and now the arcane "Science" behind it all:)

While legions of linear & transverse vectors
swerve and veer
hot-so toward the Big Zero, meat-hungry,
like bugs in a dish,
I made a secret plan for Zack
to interrupt the mythic arc
- however momentarily –
of being: Zack, just, and all, and only.
A plan to chill and engineer a little peace,
and do some more Australian Crawl
along the lonely coast of Fuego
is all I wish for, now.
Bruddahs, O-my-Bruddahs:
Not to kill, now,
but to spare,
is what I wish,
for now, and evermore.
(Pause.)
Well ... maybe so?

(Zed & Zucheo reanimate and go round & round in their
previous hassle routine. Their velocity sends them off-stage:
long-gone-away.)

(Zack spins in the water and sheds his 3-Z (minus 1) black
hat and black cowboy duster. S(h)e turns to audience
as the Mouse Van Gogh, yet again,
and now: it's that ultimate Dream-Time.)

Mouse Van Gogh
Then. I turn around.
It's all erased.
It's all edge, again.
A swarm of butterflies.
This plain Mouse, plain transmogrified.
Edge to Edge to Edge.

(Slide: Aqua-Marine Angel appears on Funky Screen.)
(MVG gazes up at Aqua-Marine Angel & Sighs.)

"Every day, it's a'gettin' closer"
Way up there, my sea, my heart.
O-Angel-Of-Surf-And-Surge,
I am liberated from the Chair.
Not to kill, now,
but to spare,
now, and ever-more-so

**(Slide: Mystic Mythic Pristine Sistine Giant Finger beckons
toward the Mouse Van Gogh. S(h)e can not resist, moves
toward the Funky Screen, and sings:)**

Getting' Cool, now
Gettin' Stupid
Singin' Um' Yeas!
and Very Much of It

118

Was a Baby
Was a Misery
Wanta' Breathe Right
Wanta' Scream!

**(MVG erupts in Little Richard-esque howl and touches
the Mystic Pristine Sistine Giant Finger.)**

O-This is De-liria, Baby!
Surfin' the Zoom
In Zoom-time, Baby!
Big & Be-Yonding, Baby-Baby!
My Angel
My Angel-Baby
So's, it's you and me, right here, Baby
It's you and me, right there, Baby
It's our turn on the dice, right now, Baby
Our turn, my Angel
My Baby, My Own Right Now,
And ever-more-so.

(Pause. The Mouse Van Gogh winks at the audience.)

So tell me there's a Cure
For all of this.
But I won't ...

Done

Gray Sergeant

At Rise:
(Gray Sergeant slogs onto stage. Useful, willing, strong, shrewd
enough to survive his own default taboos and compulsions. He
lugs his ol' kit bag behind him. He drags his role and his mission
like a ball and chain. He sweats proudly, and maintains his mode
of primed, maximal vigilance while he slogs, sweats and lugs.)

(Collapsible Tina hides quietly in Gray's ol' kit bag. Initially, s(h)e
is airless and limp. S(h)e wears a red silk kimono tied with a cord.
S(h)e also wears "the Ruby Slippers" which may be clicked
together for a change in ambience or tone. As Gray Sergeant
declaims, Collapsible Tina inflates. Eventually, s(h)e crosses an
event horizon and their situations conflate and connect.
But only briefly.)

(Gray Sergeant stops his trudge Stage-Center.
He hitches himself up – repeatedly throughout – and declaims. He
alternates props like: the Special Mouth, the Death-Wig, and his
New-New Eyes, etc. as necessary.
The Big Ol' Hands don't go on and off.)

(Gray Sergeant drops his ol' Kit Bag, grabs his Special Mouth,
Death-Wig and New-New Eyes to use as needed. He faces front,
cracks a painful smile and sings his wilderness.)

(Inside the ol' Kit Bag, Collapsible Tina lurks
and inflates, lurks and inflates, some more.)

(Gray Sergeant always holds up his Special Mouth to say
his official name / unless interrupted by Collapsible Tina.)

121

Gray Sergeant
I am Gray Sergeant,
Gray Sergeant, I am
Gray
Sergeant

**(Gray Sergeant lowers Special Mouth and points to prop
when he refers to his Special Mouth.
He always proclaims his official name
through his Special Mouth.)**

I have my **Special Mouth**
To speak:
(Gray Sergeant speaks through his Special Mouth again.)

I am Gray
Sergeant
I am
Gray

(Gray Sergeant speaks through then lowers his Special Mouth.)

I have a Special Mouth
To speak

(Gray Sergeant pops-on his Death Wig.)

I have a Death-Wig
to wear
to warm my head
when I walk
like a big man
through the big ol' shadows

**(Gray Sergeant pop-off his Death Wig and
pops-on his New-New Eyes.)**

122

I have New-New Eyes
To watch

**(Gray Sergeant pops-off his New-New Eyes.
Now he pumps & flexes: showing off his goods.)**

I have big-ol'-hands
this one I call
Blue & Bruiser
This other one's
The goddamn Golden Pig Express

(Gray Sergeant speaks through his **Special Mouth.)**

I have a Special Mouth
I
Am
Gray Sergeant

**Gray Sergeant lowers his Special Mouth.
Again, he pumps & flexes.)**

I have big-ol'-hands

(Gray Sergeant pops-on his Death Wig.)

On my head
I have a Death-Wig
to wear when I walk
down the scary red road
down the scary black road
down the eerie last road
in the shadows

(Gray Sergeant pops-off his Death-Wig and

pops-on his New-New Eyes.)

I have New-
New Eyes
to watch
my New Eyes tell me:
watch
the ocean
my New eyes tell me
watch
the air
for evidence
of juice
of rage in the rear
my New Eyes tell me:
Hell's Bells
my New Eyes tell me
juice
and rage
are evidence
enough for

(Gray Sergeant speaks through his Special Mouth)

Gray
Sergeant

(Gray Sergeant shape-shifts into "The Shooter.")

My New Eyes tell me
rage
is my ride
only,
always
like an arrow
straight atcha'

124

(Gray Sergeant shifts back. He pumps/flexes again.)

Killer
Slugger
Shank
"my own eyes ain't blank"
I have a Special Mouth
to speak:

(Gray Sergeant speaks through his Special Mouth.)

I am
Gray
Sergeant:
New Gray, New Eyes
New-New Big Ol' Hands

(Gray Sergeant lowers his Special Mouth.
He pops-on his Death Wig.
He leaves his New-New Eyes in place on his face.)

New
Gray
Death-Wig
sloggin' through shadow

(Gray Sergeant pauses. He ratchets up his resolution.)

I watch the sea
I watch the skies
I will not disremember
The evidence
Of my New-
New Eyes

(Suddenly for Gray, though we've all been watching the process,
Collapsible Tina inflates fully and their inner game is on.)

Collapsible Tina
(From behind Gray Sergeant:)
Gray
O-Gray
O-You-Gray-Meat-Baby,
You!

(Gray Sergeant wigs-big in dismay.)

Gray Sergeant
Tina!
Jesus, not here!
Not now!

(Collapsible Tina removes Gray Sergeant's New-New Eyes
abruptly, from behind.)

Collapsible Tina
Oh Yeah?
Then When?

Gray Sergeant
Not Now!
No Way!

Collapsible Tina
Yes Way!
Yes Now!

(Collapsible Tina moves in, more purposefully, on Gray Sergeant.)

Gray Sergeant
Not! – Not! – Not! – Not!

Not Now!

Collapsible Tina
Not Now.
Not Then.
No Way – No Way – Never!
So When, Gray Baby?
When?

Gray Sergeant
I
I ... don't know when.
Look, it doesn't fit Now.
Can't you wait 'til later?
Then, then ... you can ...
... we can ...
... you know ...
... then ...

Collapsible Tina
(While s(h)e fools around with Gray's Blue Bruiser &
His Golden Pig Express, S(h)e croons and bubbles.)

Then / Shmen
Look at me, Gray
you Buddha-bear
it won't fit then
no more than before:
you wait / you wait
I wig / I wig
... and you wig too.

Gray Sergeant
I?
Wig?
No Way!

127

Collapsible Tina
Yes,
Way.
Again.
See:

(Collapsible Tina takes a big breath & uncorks a long, suppurating sigh.)

You wait, you rage, you shatter.
And eventually, you wig.
Big Boo-Boo!
Big Boo-Hoo, Gray!

Gray Sergeant
Don't Say That!
It's my ... er, **(Big Whisper)** ... our secret.

(Gray Sergeant lifts up his Special Mouth to speak.)

I am:
Gray
Sergeant!

Collapsible Tina
Yeah, Yeah!
No more than before.

**(Collapsible Tina slowly pulls down
Gray Sergeant's Special Mouth.)**

Gray-Meat Baby, don't you wish?
I mean, don't you just wish
that once

you fit
inside your own skin?
Huh?

Gray Sergeant
Fit?
What Fit?

**(Gray Sergeant pops-on appropriate props as he flips – a tad
desperately – through his rolodex of attributes, assumed identities
and other protective coloration.)**

I have New-New Eyes
I have a Death-Wig to wear
I have Big-Ol'-Hands
Blue, Bruiser
Goddamn Pig Ex ...
(Pause.)
What Fit?

**(Collapsible Tina does wonderful things to Gray Sergeant with
her/ his kimono, silk cord, un-bruiser-ish hands, etc. as s(h)e talks.
S(h)e also clicks the Ruby Slippers
to punctuate and sculpt the flow.)**

Collapsible Tina
What?
Fit?
And O-What-Fit?
Like ... Fit-Fit, dontcha' know
Like Fit and deep as a fiddle.
Like Fit – to be all tied up.
Like a hand inside
a soft, silk glove:
it goes in
and it just fits.

129

Like the sublime fit
of noose
to need.
Like if the Ruby Slipper fits ya'
Buster,
shake your moneymaker
hard and
Now-now-now!

Gray Sergeant
Fit?
Fit?
I spit on fit.
I make the noose I need
Every time ...

(Gray Sergeant speaks through his Special Mouth.)

I am:
Gray
Serg ...

(Collapsible Tina pulls down
Gray Sergeant's Special Mouth, again.)

Collapsible Tina
You need Fit like you need Another Skin
inside
New Fit
an even Newer, Better Skin
New – Hip –
or nothing
Dontcha' know?

(As Collapsible Tina gets closer to his core, Gray Sergeant
reverts, again, to trudge-mode.)

130

Gray Sergeant
I have Big-Ol'-Hands
(Pause.)
Blue
Goddamn
Golden
Nothing
Fits
I Need ...

**(Collapsible Tina holds Gray Sergeant, sways him back and forth
like a dance, and talks him into her / his trance.)**

Collapsible Tina
You
Need:
Some kinda' Newer Fit
O-diggit
You-Neo-Hippus
You
got to Do to Do to Do
And *You*
got to Need it, too.

(Pause.)
**(Collapsible Tina clicks the Ruby Slippers
together again with great portent:
this tune's tone's a'gonna' change, precisely, now:)**

Remember?
That One Year?
When the Outside pushed Inside
And Everyone Inside pushed Back?
Through the holy skin of the whole world
- in a blink! -

131

Then
Stars!
Stars Everywhere!

**(Pause. Collapsible Tina guides Gray Sergeant's POV
through a cascade of stars, everywhere!
Gray sees them, too, he can't deny it.)**

Stars!
See?

Gray Sergeant
I
See
(Pause.)
I have ...
**(Gray Sergeant pops on his New-New Eyes to regain his
toxic equilibrium.)**
... New-
New Eyes
I have ...

**(Collapsible Tina jams a few nuanced fingers
into Gray Sergeant's not-so-special,
now, very ordinary standard issue mouth.)**

Collapsible Tina
Taste
my Dreamgun
wail
and cool
and dream you – Now! - upon it
Gray-baby ...

**(Collapsible Tina clicks the Ruby Slippers
while s(h)e conjures the dream.)**

132

... Dream
Dream
Dream
Sweet Gray-Baby
Dream:
Where Skin Rolls
Wet and Holy
All the Orgone Cradles
Rock-out
and It's Moon
Alone
Moon
and *Mine*
Mine
Tonight!

(With one last resonating click of the Ruby Slippers, Collapsible Tina cues a suitable tune. Sometimes s(h)e summons Harry James / Bunny Berrigan's version of "I Can't Get Started" or sometimes it's the blue-eyed "Chairman of the Board," himself, crooning "Strangers in the Night," run through a pitch-changer, at variable speeds, or something else, a few verses, just enough for a couple of major spins around the stage.
Of course, Collapsible Tina leads.)

(While Gray Sergeant and Collapsible Tina work out, a nervous giggle track overlays the music, and tension builds inside the Ol' Gray Sergeant.)

(As predicted by Collapsible Tina, Gray Sergeant wigs big. His "rage in the rear" penetrates, twists and stops the music. He also stops Collapsible Tina in her / his tracks next to the ol' Kit Bag.)

(Gray Sergeant speaks and pops-on appropriate props
while he says his mantra to make scary things – like *"Who
Do You Love?"* - disappear.)

Gray Sergeant
Fit!
Fit!
Hah, what Fit?
I have a Death-Wig
to wear
I have
New-New Eyes
I have Big-Ol'-Hands:
Bruiser, Blue
Golden Pig Express
-   right at *You!* –
Special Mouth
Too
I am Gray:
Sergeant.
Everytime
I make the Noose
I need.

Collapsible Tina
(Sad that S(h)e's losing Gray,
and sad that Gray is losing too.)
Not Good
Gray.
You Miss
All the Time.
You Watch:
The Air
You Watch
Gonna' Whirl You
Like a Sea.

134

(Gray Sergeant pops Collapsible Tina's "balloon."
Collapsible Tina melts and wriggles back into the ol' Kit
Bag.)

Gray Sergeant
I have:
Bruiser
Blue
Pig
I have a Death-
Wig

(Collapsible Tina leaks air and speaks –
sounding more and more like a dissociated droid.)

Collapsible Tina
Same Air
Same Sea
Gray.
You can't lose it.
You can't lose it.
You can't make it
go away.

Gray Sergeant
I have a Special Mouth
To speak: I am
Gray
Sergeant.

Collapsible Tina
(In a way-gone eerie timbre:)
Gray
Gray.
Can't run

away ...

(Gray Sergeant settles back into his default trudge mode.
He assumes his first position. He drags his ol' Kit Bag. He
wears all his props. Trudging off, he sweats, he strains, he
cracks a painful smile as he trudges.)

Gray Sergeant
I am Gray Sergeant
Gray
Sergeant, I am
Gray Sergeant

(Gray Sergeant drops his Special Mouth. He looks for it –
briefly in panic mode - but he can't find it. He's confused,
he's resigned, he's knee-deep in the muck of his life: way
deeper into it than he ever wanted to be.
Or conceived, even he could.)

You can't Beat Me.
You can't Be Me.
You can't Kill Me.
You can't Free Me
from the evidence
of my New-New Eyes.

Done

Hoot Cootie: a Clown Show

"In which a Plunker
Zooms A Red Bug:
With Relative Impunity"

Cast:

Red Bug: A Red Bug. Wears *Black Plastic Garbage Bag for Squishy Bones & Various Appendages. A Couple of Antennae. Some Spots*, maybe. Various *Soft Rubba' Neon-Emblazoned Body Parts* protrude from his *Black Bone Bag*. The *Standard Fresh Fur Wha-Wha* is a Real *Fur Wha-Wha*. The *Pile of New-New Threads* consists of several <u>Identical Riffs</u> on the Bug's original *Black Plastic Bag for Squishy Bone & Various Appendages.*

Plunker: A Plunker. Wears *Loin Cloth, Ankle Shells, Cowboy Hat* & *Tasty Shade*s that also function as *Gaga Omniscient Googles of Doom & Static*. Operates ancient *Kodak "Sure-Shot"* and *Polaroid* cameras with equal ease. *Seltzer Bottle* contains *Real Seltzer.*

The Rig is *Real* too. The *Dynamite Cigar* looks more pyrotechnic than Cubano.

Fresh Fur Wha-Wha technique and protocols for *"doing S-S-Suulltry"* are based on current industry standards.

Both Red Bug & Plunker are neither gender nor species specific.

Set: Anywhere with adequate lighting.

Time: It's all around us - Anytime.

At Rise:

(Lights Up – strong, sharp quick. Red Bug startles, cups, cowers. Plunker on top of box, chair, ladder, or ... Plunker points down at the Red Bug.)

Plunker
Looky - dat'- dere'. You're a Red Bug.
(Pause.) A Re-e-e-d Bug.
(Pause.) You know, you're a Red Bug.

(Plunker jumps down to Bug level. Plunker moves around the Bug as it speaks, testing the air between them for leverage.)

Red Bug
I'm a Red Bug.

Plunker
Yeah, Red Bug. Don't ask.

Red Bug
Don't Ask?

Plunker
Don't ask, that's right. You're a Red Bug.

Red Bug
Don't ask, don't ask. You're a Red Bug.

Plunker
You're a Bug!

Red Bug
I'm a Red Bug!

Plunker

Bug, you Got it! Bug for sure. And formerly, one more bug inside a sea of Red-Red Bugs – a mere hiccup in the Maw of the Cosmos. But, no more. But, not now. And soon-soon to be: *El Senor Hombre Red Bug*. Bad & Flash. More than Mere. The Verge of Red. The Edge of Legend. Stone to the Bone.
(Pause.) Think about it, Red. Bug.

Red Bug
I'm a Red Bug.

Plunker
You got it!

Red Bug
Not a hiccup! Not a Dumb Red Stone!

Plunker
No Way: Red Bug!

**(Plunker paces, jives a bit & cooks up next move.
Red Bug trails behind and yammers.)**

Red Bug
I'm a Red Bug.

Plunker
Red Bug, yeah.

Red Bug
Bug. Me. Red-Red-Red!

Plunker
Bug, you got it. You're a Red Bug. Don't! Ask!

139

Red Bug
Don't ask?

Plunker
Don't ask. You Red Bug, Red Bug, Cute little Red Bug, You.
Nothing. But. A Red-Red Bug.

Red Bug
Just a Red Bug.

Plunker
Bug, you got it! You. Are. A Red Bug. **(Pause.)** But tell you what:
You a Red Bug with some New Stuff Comin'. You 'bout to be a
better Class ... of Bug.

Red Bug
Better? Bug?

Plunker
Better Bug, Uh-Huh!

Red Bug
Better? Red? Bug?

Plunker
Bug, you got it! Still Red, but Better.
Mad & Splash.
New, and Totally!
You 'bout to be Bo-Dacious. A Better Red-Red Bug.

Red Bug
Better? How Better?

Plunker
Eyes & Ears.

140

Red Bug
Better Bug?

Plunker
Don't ask. Listen.

Red Bug
What to do?

Plunker
Look hard.

Red Bug
Look? Hard?

Plunker
Do It! Listen up: Strut that Skin like a Red Bug thinks s(h)e owns
it!

**(Red Bug does Stutter-Strut-Step. Blues or Jaw Harp
always comps the Stutter-Strut-Step.)**

Plunker
(Laughs.)
No 'bout–a-doubt it! You are a Re-e-e-e-d Bug!

Red Bug
(Red Bug Stutter-Strut-Steps & talks, simultaneously.)
I'm a Red Bug.

Plunker
(Plunker Jives, Jitters & Scats.)
Yeah, yeah, you 'bout got it. Red. Bug.

Red Bug
I'm a Re-e-e-e-e-d / Bug!

(Plunker interrupts at /.)

Plunker

Listen up ... Red Bug. First Ima' gonna' throw you Smoke.
All around. Then I throw you new stuff you can use.
Red. Bug.

Red Bug

Don't Ask?

Plunker
(Laughs.)

You got it ... Bug. Hey, c'mere. Check out this ... Fresh ... Fur ...
Wha- Wha I got for you. Especially. It – Is – An - Attitude –
Unto. Unto you. Bug.
Go on. Try out your very own Fresh Fur Wha-Wha.

(Red Bug shows No Clue.
So Plunker demos *Standard*
*Fresh Fur Wha-Wha technique.***)**

Wha-Wha down. Red. Bug.
(Plunker lays the *Standard Fresh Fur Wha-Wha* **upon the Red Bug.**
Red Bug also *Wha-Wha's down.* **And** *Stutter-Strut-Steps,*
simultaneously.)

Red Bug

Wha ... Wha ... Down.

Plunker
(Laughs & Claps.)

Bug, you gotta' work that Wha & Walk together!
Bug, you gonna' learn to Walk like a Prince!
(Pause.)
Among Red Bugs.

142

(Red Bug Works the Wha & Stutter-Strut Step, together.)

That's Better, Bug.

Red Bug
(Still Wha-Stutter-Strut-Steppin'.)
Better?

Plunker
Hey. You're gettin' Better all the time.
For a Bug.

Bug
I'm a Red ... Bug.

Plunker
You are the Boss: Red ... Bug!

Red Bug
(Fully Synched & full of her / his Buggy Suchness.)
I-am-the-Reddest-Reddest-Reddest
Reddest-Red-Red Bug.

Plunker
Whoa down.. Trust me, Bug. This AIN'T your Last Life. No More
Crawlin' ... inside the drain ... Bug versus Bug. Upon the Floor. You
are ... **(BIG!)** ... no More...
You are: Li-Ber-Ate-'d from IT.

**(Red Bug Beams & Wha-Wha-Stutter-Strut-Steps
a few more licks.)**

Point-of-Fact, Bug, It's Gone for Good. And Ye, me' Bug-O, shall
Hence-Forth, and Permanently, Inhabit a State of Way-Goneness:
Like unto Clear White Light. Strong & Pure, Bug.

143

(Plunker spews her / his pitch and bops over toward Pile of New-New Threads for the next operation.)

(While Plunker riffs on the essence of Self-Transformation and subsequent Gone—ness, the Red Bug looks back and forth between his own Squishy Bone Bag and the Pile of New-New Threads, and scopes the New Threads-Old Threads total congruence. Red Bug does tentative Stutter-Strut-Steps and tries a few feeble Wha's. But whenever the Red Bug tugs on the Plunker, the Plunker flicks her / him off – Like A Bug!)

Believe me, Bug. It's a New Regime. Look hard cuz' you got you a Choice of 10 ... I say 10 ... Unbelievable! ... (Plunker throws Black Plastic Squishy Bone & Appendage Bags up in the air like leaves) ... Absolutely Original Squishy Bone Bags ... with holes ... for squishy bones ... and various other Appendages you might find ... on a Bug! One. For Each. Leg. Or other Thing. Hey!!! Let's DO IT!!!

(Plunker – Unceremoniously – Rips off Bug's Old Bag. Bug's Guts (and Other Things) Protrude, Wiggle, Crawl, etc. The Plunker Gags and does the Ol' Death-Wig Horror with hands, eyes, etc.)

Gawd!!! Yuck!!! What the Hell have you been Eatin' on, Bug!

Red Bug
(With Pride.)
Don't ask. I. Am. A Red Bug.

Plunker
Yeah, yeah. Don't ask. I can dig it, Bug.
But the Groove you got is sure enough, Stanky.
That's some kinda' 'Arfel 'Bomination, Bug.

(Plunker POPS a new Bag on the Bug.)

Whew!! That was a hair too close to this cat's
Zone of Meltdown, in totality!!

**(Plunker Removes & then Re-Applies her / his Gaga Omniscient
Goggles of Doom & Static, with Deep Ceremony – and Precision.)**

Glad I wear my Gaga Omniscient Goggles of Doom & Static ... like
a True Religion!!

(Arms wide, Plunker Scopes the "New" Red Bug.)

Now! 'Dat's Meow!! 'Dat's ... Killer-Killer!!
Bug. You are now: a True Pro!!
(Plunker kneels at the feet of the Red Bug.)
Behold ... The Bug!!

(Plunker rises, Pats Bug on the Back.)

My Bud, the Bug. An. Attitude. Unto.
A Veritable Buddha. Of True Bamboozlement.

**(Plunker Pats the Bug again. Stops.
Pats Bug, again, Harder. Stops.)**

Wait – a – Minute?
(Plunker Pokes the Red Bug.)

Red Bug
OOOWWW!

Plunker
This Bug ain't got Nooooo Bone.

(Plunker Pokes Bug, again.)

Red Bug
OOOWWWW!!

Plunker
WoooWeeee! Checkidout!
This little Red Bug ain't got Nooooo Bone.

**(Plunker "Gumbee's" Red Bug to show Inherent Flexion:
2 or 3 postures does it up right.)**

You a Pwetty Twicky Bug.
For a Bug, ... Bug.
(Pause.)
But don't let it bug you, 'cuz:
stretched out or snug,
fulla' piss or fulla' rubba'
Bug to the Bone or ...

(Plunker Pokes the Red Bug, again.)

Red Bug
OOOOWWWWW!!!

Plunker
... NOT!
You are still Primo Fino!
An Energetic, Embryonic/Enthusiastic, People-Sort-of-Bug
who enjoys ...

**(Red Bug Forays down to Work the Crowd
& Show what s(h)e's told on-cue.
But it's all Greek (or geek) to a Red Bug.)**

... Meeting, Greeting, Tweeting & Bleating ...
... "Fine Dining" on the right occasion.
And never whines about the vintage, or the bite.

Tah-Dah!!

**(The Red Bug Droops, Shrugs,
Goes All Random for a moment.)**

Red Bug
Red Bug? Don't Ask? What to Do ...
What To / Do?

Plunker
Whoa-on Down There, Bug.
Lighten up. Don't Blubber, Bug. Don't Despair.
Boneless ... or not ... your New Bag comes ... Tah! Dah! ...
with Tasty Shades.

**(Plunker tries a few Tasty Shades on the Red Bug, *muy rapido*.
Hey! They're all the same!)**

One to Suit. Your Own. Personal. Whim – or – Scam.

(Plunker Frames the Red Bug with her / his hands.)

Cool!! Ultra!!
Time for Pix, Red Bug.

**(Plunker whips out Sure Shot camera and rapid fires.
Bug Cups, Cringes, Cowers BUT tries to show
something like what Plunker asks for.)**

Yeas! I say Yeas!
Your Bug-ness, you are Soooooo!! Hot!!
Now show Full. Shoe. Frontal Lobe.
And Lip.
(Plunker gets a new idea!)
Say! You need a little sweat to Show you're greased to Go!

147

(Plunker Sprays the Red Bug in face with Seltzer.)

Red Bug
Whaa!! Whaa!!

Plunker
OOOO!! A Wha from the Heart.
I-Con-O-Graphic, Dontcha' Know.
Tell you what, Red ... Bug, that's a Whaa you can travel on.
Tasty!! O-So-Very-Very Tasty!!
(Pause.)
Now. Show SUUULLTRY, Bug. Show Some Steam.
Flex Yer' Fur. Give it up, Bug!! Tah-Dah!!

(Red Bug Droops, Shrugs, Goes Random, once again.)

Red Bug
Whaa!! Whaa!!

Plunker
Lose the Wha, Bug. Show us, don't Preach us Raw.
C'mon: Sultry, Bug, Suuulltry!
(Pause. Plunker Shows Suuulltry.)
Here. S-S-Suuullltry. This-a-way.
Lick your lip.
Need some sweat to set the mood?
**(Plunker sprays the Red Bug in face
with Seltzer, again.)**

Red Bug
Whhaa!!! WHHAA!!!

Plunker
That Whaa has got to Go, Bug! *Mira!*
(Plunker does Sultry, again.)
Here. S-S-Suulltry! This way. Stick it out.

148

This way ... lick your lip.
Need some sweat to get all slippery,
My Bug-a-Boo, Mis-Tah Hippery?
(Plunker spray Bug in Face again with Seltzer.)
Nooo-Problema!

Red Bug
Whhhaaa!!! Whhhaaa!!!

Plunker
Don't wear out your Whaa, Bug.
Whaa's an ace, not a caboose.
Now: Sultry.

(Red Bug Tries Sultry, again.)

C'mon. S-S-Suulll-try. Do It!!

(PLunker pokes the Red Bug, again.)

Red Bug
OOOWWW!!!

Plunker
Yeah-Yeah-Yeah!!! Ultissimo, Bug.
Sufferin' Sultries, what a Killer-Move.
Oh-You-Are: a Solid. Solid. Suffra', Bug-Baby.
You. Are. An Uber-Bug.
If One Bug ever was. One? Bug?

Red Bug
I'm a Red Bug

Plunker
You got it. You Are A Get-Down Bug, Bug.
& Down for it, two times more, already.

And – NOW! - You-Are-Ready-For-It!

Red Bug
It?

Plunker
Don't Ask.

Red Bug
Don't Ask?

Plunker
So Now you got IT, Bug!
So Now you got to give IT up!

(Red Bug Does S-S-Suulltry.)

A Look. A Walk.

(Red Bug does S-S-Suulltry, Whaa-Whaa Down & Stutter-Strut-Steppin', simultaneously.)

(Plunker Laughs.)
O-Killer-Killer. You are now ready for a line. Of vacant.
And Arranged. Smoke & Hyper-Zine babble, Gene.
To fill the time on your hands ...
**(Plunker takes Bug Appendage in his own hand,
Shudders Ferociously, and Drops it.)**
... or whatever.

(Plunker Waxes Big & Expansive ...)
O Bug of Elegance!
O Bug of Taste & Leisure!
O Arbiter of Science Stuff & Economic Stratagems, too!
Talk to Me!

150

Red Bug
I'm a Red Bug.

(Plunker Whacks his own forehead.)

Yeah. Right. A Cool Fool, no doubt.
(Pause.)
Listen up, Bug. This here's the Zen part. Float-Scatter, Dice &
Splice. Recombine. Like the GENE POLICE do. Without visible
effort. Without attachment, that's the Main Thing: Each phrase
Tics from Tongue to Lips.
The line won't fly if it ain't got Swing.

Red Bug
Swing?

Plunker
Don't Ask.

Red Bug
Don't Ask?

Plunker
You got it. Listen. There's a Code. And a Theme.
Weave around it. Blur Big, then Swoop. Say What I Say.
Develop some fine Veee-LAAHH-City. Scope me, then Scoop me.
You. Can. Do. It. Listen:

(Plunker Riffs Solo:)

ZEIT GEIST
ZELLAGUBA
ZEM-ZEM
ZARATHUSTRA

(Plunker TO Bug.)

151

YOU DIG? YOU do. Now. With me.

Red Rug
Don't Ask?

Plunker
You Got it! Jam-On-It!

Plunker & Red Bug
(Together, though Red Bug has some Major problems.)
DEMI-MONDE
DELECATO
DOPPLEGANGER
DUPE-SNOOT

Plunker
Not bad fer' a Bug. Or a Rogue Tongue with Chill Intent.
Now we gonna' go for Ignition. Velocity. Thrust & Bore.
C'Mon, show us some Speed, Keed!!

Plunker & Red Bug
PONCABRATOR
WELTA-A-ANSHA-U-U-UNG
ZAUM-MEISTER
"KASAVUBU"

**(That session turns out bad for the Bug.
So Plunker Inspects the Red Bug's tongue
while s(h)e does the next pitch.)**

Plunker
Extra-Ordinary! Both Fey & Subtle, Bug.
Now! Punch Up Scramble! Scat-Scat!!
Function at the Junction!
Too Little Too Late Too Much Too Bad – Badder - Baddest!!!
Let 'Ar Blow!!!

152

Plunker & Red Bug
**(While Plunker Scats & Scrambles, the Red Bug Stares, Scratches,
goes briefly Random, stumbles on the words.)**
HAUTE KULTUR
RHIZOMATIC
ZHO-RA DORA
HAUTE COIFFURE

Plunker
C'Mon Red Bug: Dig, Blow,
Scramble them Morphemes.

Plunker & Red Bug
HOOT COOLIE
HOOT COOLIE

Plunker
Bug! Energize!! Ignite!!
Skin yourself, your own Self, and Mash it all together!!
Do IT!! Do IT!!!

(Plunker pokes the Bug, again.)

Red Bug
OOWW!!

Plunker & Red Bug
HOOT COOTIE
HOOT COOTIE

**(No time for the Red Bug to think about it. Plunker pokes the Bug
again to regroup for the Ultimate Blow-Off.)**

Red Bug
OOOWWW!!!

153

(Plunker takers a deep breath. The Red Bug does so, too. Plunker
starts to BUZZZZZZZZ. Bug does, also.
Together, they jam entire list.
Tough, again for the Red Bug.)

Plunker & Red Bug
(ZZZZZZZZZZZZZZ)
ZEIT GEIST
ZELLAGUBA
ZEM-ZEM
ZARARTHUSTRA
DEMI-MONDE
DELECATO
DOPPLEGANGER
DUPE-SNOOT
PONCABRATOR
WELT-A-A-ANSHAU-U-U-UNG
ZAUM-MEISTER
"KASAVUBU"
HAUTE KULTUR
RHIZOMATIC
ZHO-RA DORA
HAUTE COIFFURE

(Big & Bigger!)

HOOT COOLIE!
HOOT COOTIE!!
HOOT COOTIE!!

(Biggest!)

HOOT COOTIE!!!

Plunker

Zing! Bam!! You are now a Crash Culture Operator, Bug!!
(Plunker Chants:) HOOT COOTIE - HOOT COOTIE - HOOT
COOTIE - HOOT COOTIE ... **(Less of a PAUSE, more of a
Screeching Halt.)** A True Boss-Tone from the Fetid Heart of the
Zone of Unlove. O-Hoot Cootie, O-Bug-O-Mine. You make it
New, Viii-Brationally Speaking, each time you intone: Hoot Cootie
... Hoot Cootie. Can YOU scope the Possibilities? Does it Snag
You? Bug?

Red Bug
I'm a Red Bug?

Plunker

Red, Red and so much more. Hoot Cootie. Gonna'-Gonna' WOW
the Town with SMOKE-SMOKE-SMOKE: You are the Bare-Ass
Rabble-Meister of Giga-Watt Stomp, in full Pomp. And, also, fully
Psycho: Hoot Cootie. Hoot Cootie! Don't you see? Now you can
be FULL-FULL-FULL ... and EMPTY. Simultaneously.

Red Bug
I'm a Red Bug?

Plunker

Don't ASK, Bruddah Hoot! Now You Drift & Dance & YOU
control every Circumstance. Full & Empty. That's the Key. Full &
Empty. You See IT? So let the Slovaks Shudder in their Drawers.

Red Bug
Don't Ask?

Plunker
You Got IT! You just Chill. And Wait.
I'll go percolate the pix.
(Plunker flourishes the ancient Polaroid Camera.)
I'll make you up a package you can use.

155

(Plunker Stops & Scopes the Red Bug
in her / his mythic entirety.)
Hoot Cootie! Hoot Cootie!
What a Bug! What a Bug!
What a Fine Red Bug YOU Are!!
(Plunker PAUSES – with Pride.)
You'll do it up Right. And Proud.
'Til Bye-Bye. 'Til Good-Nighty-Night!
And in rolls YOUR Very Own: Cyanide PIE!!!

Red Bug
Pie?

Plunker
Pie. Some treat, indeedy, Me' Bug-O!

Red Bug
Don't Ask?

Plunker
You Got IT! For now, YOU're a Fine Bug.
Born Free. And S-S-Suulltry!

**(Red Bug snaps back into "doing S-S-Suulltry."
Plunker snaps the Bug's move with the ancient Polaroid.)**
Plunker
Here ...
**(They both watch as the Polaroid spews out
Undeveloped Red Bug photo.)**
... Watch Yourself Appear ...
(Plunker points to Undeveloped Photo.)
... Right here. The Center of Your EYE.
Until ... You know ... PIE.

Red Bug
BYE-BYE!!

Plunker
YOU GOT IT!!!

Red Bug
(Red Bug points to the blank photo.)
Red Bug?

Plunker
Red Bug's a-comin in its own good time.
Simulacrum-City. Rat' 'Chere.
Just Chill. And Wait.
It's Positive and almost – Sort of –
Instantaneous Re-In-Farce-ment.
(Pause.)
After All. You are Just ...
(Plunker Pokes Bug, again.)

Red Bug
OOOWWW!!!

Plunker
A Red ...

(Plunker Pokes Bug, yet again.)

Red Bug
OOOOWWWW!!!!

Plunker
Say Bug, later on. Squeeze one for me.
At your ease and only if YOU please.
... And here's the Clincher: a Dynamite Cigar ...

157

(Plunker Pops the Dynamite Cigar
between the Red Bug's mandibles.
Tosses the Rig at Red Bug's feet.)
And, too ... and Also ... your very own
POISONAL Rig. Can YOU Dig IT?
Later-Later, O-Bug-of-the HEMISPHERE!
Here's Zoomin'!! YOU!!

(Plunker Strolls off. Slow. Always Weird. Sometimes Backwards.
And Spews a welter of motivational aphorisms (and such-like) as
s(h)e Strolls.)

Work the WHAA & the Walk. Sufferin' S-S-S-uulltries!
Zarathustra-Killer-Move! Iconize da' Whaa!
Veee- Locity! Veee-Locity! Show us some Speed, Keed!
Tic-Toc / Tic-Toc. 'Da Groove is Ulterior!
Zaum-Meister. Scatter-Float. Mambo. Recombine.
Dice & Slice, O-Uber-Bug, THE MULTIVERSE is Thine.
Sufferin' – Sufferin' – S-S-S-uulltries!
Moot-Hoot: Is Hoot merely Moot? Or No? Or Maybe So?
Papa Legba. Papa Legba.
O-YOU-SOUL-SOUL-SAPPA'!!
Papa-OOO-Mau-Mau!
And. And. And Sky.

(Plunker is no where to be seen, now. Red Bug picks up the Rig.
S(h)e sits down, squirts it, plays with it, then tosses it away. Bug
crosses legs, picks up ancient Polaroid and Watches with Focus as
an Image-of-the-Bug Appears. Bug's face Lights UP. Bug stands,
adjusts the Fresh Fur Whaa-Whaa, holds photo out like s(h)e's
taking a selfie, or, most probably, using it like a model-mirror for
the next Move. The Red Bug "does S-S-Suulltry.")

(Red Bug doesn't get it right. Stops. Tries again.
Red Bug doesn't get it right. Stops. Tries again ...
Red Bug doesn't get it right. Stops. Tries ...)

Ishtar Over Berkeley: A Choreo-Poem, a Ghost Sutra, a Talk & Worry Routine

*"How do we get back to the beginning, to perfection,
to the origin of our blood, to paradise new?"*
—Juan Felipe Herrera

Voices:
Blue Woman, 3rd Person, Mute (but Not)
Blue Woman's Lost Man
Bone Moon, Possibly a Ghost
Blue Woman's Last Man
Frankie. This Striving-Craving Bad-Ass
Woman's Very Best Machine
Ghost Chorus in the Aethers, Possibly Aldebaran Talking
Jive Buddha/Tiresias, Possibly a Ghost

(Setting: On the street, at night, in fog. Begins at the corner of Telegraph Ave. and Dwight Way. Berkeley, California, as once and future Theatrum Mundi.)

(Blue Woman's Lost Man:)

Where my feet are, that's what it always starts with:

Drag down the Murder Tree, reload
a deep hot kiss, a revolutionary widening

161

of the heart and eye, a third trumpet
wails out its blue dirge, a burning star
falls into the River of Life,
and drags me past speechless, through
merely silent, dancing
backward, toward Ishtar

(dancing backward to remember
where my feet have been,
if I only danced forward
I could only forget) where ...

"to embody and ensoul what's actual"
to sift this sticky fog for signs,
mutations / distortions: nucleic states
encoded in sound, gesture, scuffle, stage
directions for a chorus of unruly ghosts,
in faint dust falling from Aldebaran,
like sweet anesthesia over Berkeley,
the juniper and manzanita hills above,
where a bone moon dreams like Ishtar
tethered to her 12th house of lips
and fishes, this tricky moon, I can't
buy into, asks me:

(Bone Moon:)

*"What can't you live without, now that
she's left you for a dream that follows
the spoor of her very own Grail?
What was your first face, from your body in your
last life, back-a-days, before it
locked and stiffened as your
body-in-this-too-familiar-lie?
Can you understand the mute, hear the
silent, simply by moving into it, simply*

by erring, warring, daring,
and moving into it, yet again?"

(Blue Woman's Lost Man:)

Like a ghost – a being mostly mute - I have no answer.
Like any ghost, I know, all bets are off, there
will be no dance into rapture, for me,
"done for, done for, never time enough
to finish singing," for me,
a banished son of Ishtar gone away so long
from this blue woman on her corner
of Inspiration and Self-Deception. She's
still there crooning "Come Love," like the Lady,
because she thinks blue's the color of unabashed
regret blooming next to Ishtar's soft breasts, since
her last man before me is all gone, and so
finally, she forgets to feed her roses,
now, she dusts her own breasts, her belly, her
sweet ankles and her thighs with something
blue and sweeter, yet, she still sleeps too much,
too late, with her own baby phoenix on a cloud of rue,
adrift and invisible in an ocean of disremembering,
see, her last man wracked her up, her last man
stripped her hot circuits bare, and ground them
into poison and tears, thrashed her seed
around inside her, made her high then made her
bleed clean into the next century, saying
like a murmur, deep, dark, all actorly, you know:

(This next shard of declamation is hardly on the level. The
reference to Animus is strictly sham to elevate the basest
intentions, the most self-aggrandizing will to dominate, or a dead
or absent spirit that recoils from meaning, or touch. *Defy, belie,*
***defame, betray* would, perhaps, be more authentic tonal colors for**
the actors. But didn't Jung once say that love and power are

163

shadows of each other?)

(Blue Woman's Last Man:)

"Hey my woman, my only woman, it's
the Animus talkin', it's a pale shadow
'cross my heart-thing talkin', don'tcha'
know it too good, and yet, I'm still
compelled to sin, compelled to sin,
compelled to sin, don'tcha' know ..."

(Blue Woman's Lost Man:)

so now, she never sleeps with me,
who could blame her, I might weigh her down
when, next, the sun twin comes a'knocking
on her window, when it's time to rise,
again, though the mouths of guilty mandolins,
and she rises up into that ghost-light, rises
up above the strobe and snarl and bicker
of this steady disappointment, rises up
like sweet smoke to Ishtar, and leaves me
locked-out from her Sefirot of secrets, her
glad routines of self-love, and other-earthly beauty,

and rootless, I, and once again, tongueshot,
spurned to boot, wandering our *Theatrum Mundi*
(a.k.a. Telegraph Ave.) on down toward Alcatraz
and Oakland with Frankie of the skinny arms, all
sliced and furrowed, saying always, *"Hey,*
I ain't no saint. And you ain't a' gonna'
lose me that easy," again, she extolls all
the perks of conscious derangement:
"rehearsing my very own myth, again,"
says Frankie of the cold itch,
bonejelly, yellow eyes and all, and she's

slid back hard, or so she tells it, hears
the walls, now, talking down to her,
and living in a laundromat, again,
(that's no place for a decent ghost)
but now, she's turned pro, or so she
tells it, now, this spooky moon just drips,
drips, drips and rough hands and the stiff
horn slide further up her own thighs, and
sometimes, it's a for-real badge-man
on the business end, for-real and
"of most excellent fancy," calls himself
an angel, or a mensch, objectively,
with his own fire, and his own itch,
aimed most precisely, so-so no never-mind
is he, and tonight, *twee bebe*, you have to
ride that dead mythology, again:

**(Two things we must remember, at this juncture: Jack Spicer
claimed that meaning and ghosts might mix no better than oil and
water, and when they *"converge as a signifyin' totem, they're probably
fakin' it."* The other refers to pitch, pace and timbre of the ghost
chorus: nuances derive from Albert Ayler's surveillance and
channeling of flayed, sometimes screeching, sometimes hushed,
sometimes, even, conspiratorially sonorous, recombinant ghost
babble bound together in multi-polar saxophone *corridos*.)**

(Ghost Chorus:)

*"O we own, we wile you finebone
mama, wipe your story empty from
the inside, we inject, we inject you
with a cold wire, then, raw teeth
of the Dragon - - feel him stirring up, ya tu sabes.
Hey, you feel him come'a, come'a,
stirring up the coma agents, he?
Hey you: ungrip, wild and wild awhile, eh?*

You flutter like a temblor?
Need some more to burn?
Hey you, we and we together say let's go
earn a place that's no appendage
of another's dream.
Say raise yourself, ignite
your desire, you never got to die
outside of Ishtar's grace when real
skin's looking for a pulse
to pump against, when seed
with no face a'gonna
blast out your own fire
... say, blast out your own fire.
Say it: until the coma's gone,
your own arm wakes up,
and the itch...

(Blue Woman's Lost Man:)

But you know Frankie says old Ishtar's
pretty tricky (like that moon I can't believe in):
her godface looks too cool, considering all
those eons of hard use, nothing like human shape
or form opens into her eyes, and her breath
blows beau coup fractal static into each
night's air, but, *"Hey, check her chest out,"*
says Frankie. *"See, it heaves all very*
righteous. There, it heaves again, say,
that's the need part, me and her
and you, together, go there, too."
Inside Ishtar one hot engine purrs, and
Frankie know the purrs and the how's, knows
she'll bust off her last tooth as a lustrum
for Ishtar - of the black ice skid, eternal
amputations, of nightshade and its shivers - Ishtar
of the cold wire sting, unredeemed, and so

166

she *"walkalongs and walkalongs"*
her Via Negativa, stripping back the history
of her habit, breaking every rule
of "Good Governance" with her body and her will.
She steady puts on the mileage to outrun
these ghosts but this arch moon's cool
regard, just like any other reptile's,
means zed to naught for her.
It's velocity and simple she knows
best, you got to go real fast
to keep a wreck like this in orbit
through its predestined burn time, end time,
and such, you pray from skin on into other
skin for a working metaphysic,
but you still got nothing, but itself,
a skin of nothing much, a low rent Arcana
stalled in mud, no potent *gris-gris*
just a dud for posterity, and so it comes
down to her own voice – what she knows
and more or less can trust – and she does
know what and how to roar up with her own
voice ... to the outermost habitat of Aldebaran
and the others, floating up above
this sticky fog, she roars:

(Frankie:)

*"Ishtar, you old drag-dog woman: your fire got
snuffed out, long time back, but you blinked
'cause you was stoned on suffer and surrender;
you never saw nothing, did you?
And most mornings when you woke up
you was wearing someone else's blood.
I seen you, I remember
while I drag my own skinny*

167

shroud of rags and shit and stone
distemper 'cross this pavement,
a thousand zippers open to the night
on this greedy moon's say-so, and still
your old dead tongue stays
locked inside my ear.

Hey, I know I'm cooked.
I'm burned stiff. I'm gonna' drop myself
and ... and shatter. But when I'm worn down
to my holy elements, nothing but
a cinder of my own self, only then
can I conversate
with Death and Time,
with Truth and Mercy,
and Fate.

See, I know I'm just Our Lady
of the Holy Teaspoon, steel
communal needle, busted rubber: used,
then tossed, then kicked away.
But I'm still this striving-craving bad-ass
woman's very best machine, and totally,
on-my-own elective ... until that
itch catches me up, again.

Then I got to go up above myself,
pull myself outside myself, get
these itch circuits all dusted and calm
down again, and perch outside on the outside
of the actual where a new god, half a woman,
half a man with a single shared eye, stirs
from its mortal trance, gestures me
up toward Aldebaran, whispers into me
like bum wine, so s(h)e says:

("Bum wine's" a tip off that Frankie's on to this "god." Either highly fortified "graveyard stew" (for maximum blurring of the truth), or just a common "bum steer" stratagem, again, avoiding any real dialogue with the Big T. Recall another telling detail from the ghost world, a la Jack Spicer: *"When ghosts engage in explanatory discourse, they're probably faking it, again. Ghosts don't intend to explain anything."* If, in fact ...)

(Jive Buddha / Tiresias:)

"They're coming down for us.
I see them, blue and pure land
dreaming down the way as they come.
And they laugh, too, as they come for us,
see, it's all for us, me and you, and it's
no dream really more like a picture
in the orbit of their great kind eyes.
And so are we all.
Here, touch my skin, then stroke the sky.
You can feel them cool, still distant,
and blue, and honey don't despair,
you can feel them, now, too."

(Frankie:)

"But I tell him, no, it ain't a'gonna end
like that 'cause each night's got
this sticky fog, some gray-grubby moon above,
itchy arms and zippers all around me,
frost and dust and static floating,
all around me, nothing talks straight,
leaves this hole in me that spins
away, awful, into dead orbit, into burn
down time, and raw, all around me, this
moon full of spite flat eats me up
... and they don't never come,

169

no way, just the wire,
all around me, and
they-don't-never-come.

I'm down here swimming toward the sun.

And they just send more of the wire."

The Baby's Rookie Year

*"Balance could be a bad thing, a trick to keep
you stuck in the middle where things always add up.
Where you can do no visible harm or any real, lasting
good, for that matter."*
—Naomi Wallace

1. A Back Story:

The theme of **The Baby's Rookie Year** came from the mouth of
Fairouz, a character in Naomi Wallace's play, "In the Heart of
America": *"There are three kinds of people. Those who kill. Those who
die. Those who watch. Which one are you?"* This piece is more
nuanced than Fairouz's zero-sum formula, but brevity rules here
and that's the basic gist.

I've known The Baby Rookie most of my life. We grew up together,
went to school together, drank together, fought kids from other
high schools – each running wingman for the other - and fought /
diss'ed / cussed each other out back-a-days, in the same parochial
Podunk far from any hub of imperial influence, power or culture.
We share aspects of the same cultural DNA: the same early
exposures to class prejudice, racial animus (both for and against),
twisted misconceptions of gender roles, sexual insecurities, and
groveled before the face of local-yokel power – while hissing some
regional riff on *Fuck You, Moloch!* under our breath. We were (as
others like us) effectively exiled from the vital core of the social
dynamic that pulled all our chains. The military was where our
paths diverged.

The Rookie's insignificant / negligible / completely expendable place in the grand scheme can, once again, be summarized in this terse clip of conversation from Wallace's same play. Here, Lt. Boxler grills Private Craver Perry to sleuth out and clarify details of Craver's personal history, which he can later use to reinforce the young man's insecurities, shame, and sense of worthlessness:

> Lt. Boxler: *Where are you from?*
> Craver: *Town of Hazard, Kentucky. Sir!*
> Lt. Boxler: *Let me see your teeth. Hmm! Trash, are you?*
> Craver: *Yes, Sir!*
> Lt. Boxler: *Joined up because you couldn't get a job?*
> Craver: *Yes, Sir!*

You can substitute an infinite number of place names for the "town of Hazard, Kentucky. Gallup NM, Eloy or Coolidge AZ, Vacaville CA, Joliet IL, Cleveland MS, Ponca City OK, Oil City PA, Crowley LA, Gillette WY, Edna, Winnie or Beeville TX come to mind but that's just based on my own personal experience. There are an almost infinite number of places to incubate and raise a damaged Baby Rookie. Some might call the places on this list bucolic, possibly pastoral. Some would say more like pinched and sad. Any way you cut it, the list is very long and the teeth all look the same.

The layered shame of his hereditary demographic must scream a lot inside The Rookie's head – like congenital accusations of core insufficiency and futility / like bathing in a toxic pool of Situationist self-pity. And the limits of his birthplace in space does have so much bearing on his lack of perspective, his biases and amnesias. Hey, I know he's green, deprived, under-stimulated and, ultimately, just a rube to be used and discarded. I've been there, myself, and we will all soon see exactly how and why he suffers from this quiet mind-killer / a soul sapping lack of what it takes to go forward in life. (Whatever forward might imply in this (his) context). But any claims, here, to mitigating circumstances must come across as weak / unconvincing and, ultimately, relativistic.

The Rookie is – like all of us are - personally responsible for the suffering he visits upon others. Even when it boomerangs back on him (or us) in spades. Seeing the pain he causes play out and carrying those guilty memories of the ambiguities / contradictions / levels of betrayal / and all the fake identities you must constantly manufacture and reinforce to go along just to get along makes it even worse. For him quite directly; for the rest of us through the mirror of his story.

The contrast with Tarrou, the last victim In Camus' *The Plague*, is stark. Tarrou's beliefs are uncompromising, transcendent and well-nigh impossible in this world as we have made it.

> *"I must reject everything that indirectly or directly kills people, justifies making them die, or even makes their lives so miserable they want to die."*

This strict rule deontologist's position is perhaps the most difficult ethical dead-lift imaginable. I could hardly say my own actions even come close. But I'd certainly like The Rookie to gin up some empathy and, consider something more like Tarrou's option.

Empathy and its absence is key, here, but in The Rookie's world empathy is truly an endangered species. And watching how irony / dogma / myth / and peer-culture compliance shut down the growth of empathy you have to wonder how empathy ever develops at all. The Baby Rookie's lack (or avoidance) of it and his huge case-load of personal fears have made him an odd (but fairly common) form of emotional zombie: a chronic outcast, a perpetual self-exile. His inability to engage with others and his own feelings begets a sense of futility that promotes compliance with orders and directives, that sneers at and devalues compassion, and begets complicity in atrocities and theft. That death march of the soul leads inevitably to actual approval of the principles and actions that beget domestic violence, terror, even genocide, in the pursuit of dominance: based like any program of systematic dominance must be on greed, hierarchy, cultural arrogance, misogyny and economic murder.

Without empathy and its other wing, compassion, what's left of a life, anyway?

2. Building a Composite / Making a Confession:

The core of the idea for a character like Mr. URKUMU – now there's an abstraction for you! - grew from meeting activists from the *Achuar, Kichwa (Sarayaku)* and *Zápara* peoples during their visits to Houston TX. They came to speak at annual meetings of shareholders about crimes against their land, their villages, their cultures and their health committed, most specifically by Chevron, but also by some of the lesser Texas oil-gods. One particular moment from that process is burned into my brain.

A throng of anti-fossil fuel demonstrators surged the sidewalks, bulging out into Smith Street in downtown Houston. The crowd eddied around two *Kichwa (Sarayaku)* elders in traditional dress – ceremonial face-paint, macaw feathers, bright cloth - a woman and a man. They stood at the foot of a long, very steep concrete stairway leading up to the Chevron building's entrance; they conferred with organizers from a few of the civil society groups sponsoring this action. They rearranged their position relative to the others while photos and video footage were captured for the record.

Then calmly and with maximum (and quite visible) resolve, they walked up that long set of steps toward the tall, posh-burnished steel doors at the entrance to the building. The fire-dragon Texas sun beat down unmercifully. They were flanked by close to 30 Houston police officers, at the ready / in light-riot gear. No one else walked with them. They climbed the stairs, almost in step, never looking back, until an officer opened the door, and the space

– with its high ceiling vestibule full of pricey high-dollar art swallowed them up. I thought of the massive AC units inside that building and wondered how the first frigid blast felt when it hit them.

I can imagine Mr. URUKUMU making that same long walk, but solo; in fact, that's how he first appeared on the scene in my own head. Buttressed by the living example of activist indigenous leaders like Kayapo chief, Paulinho Paiakan – who died this year during the COVID pandemic devastating their region.

Mr. URUKUMU is well cultivated, a polymath and autodidact, worldly without seeming so, and he knows quite a bit more about us and how our world works – or rather, how we've worked over our world – than we think he knows. This is his personal edge and his edge can be sharp. He's a more or less cerebral revolutionary, but with his feet on the ground, and no crippling illusions about the difficulties, contradictions and inherent messiness of systemic change. He sees through smarmy neo-liberals and self-congratulatory radicals, alike, in a glance. About fascists and imperialists, he knows enough to dodge 'em. But it's getting harder. Sometimes, I think he knows our world so much better than we do.

As for the enticements and perks of our developed world privilege, he wants and appreciates real help with things like pure water infrastructure, health care outreach, education (of a useful kind), and political air cover – if offered in a generous / non-condescending spirit, with no ulterior strings attached. But we can check our actual developed world mindset at the edge of the forest, thank you. Along with our guns, heavy earth-wrecking machines, depressions, hysterias and, especially, our lethal viruses and, often equally lethal, memory sickness.

Like so many current indigenous leaders in the Amazon, Mr. URUKUMU refuses to be victimized. Dissecting, dismantling, positively disemboweling The Baby Rookie's worldview, and groundless sense of

177

self (without prescribing remedies to "improve and temper' The Rookie's distorted ego) is Mr. URUKUMU's role in the story's rhetoric. The remedial end of that project is strictly up to The Rookie: if he's up to the project. This is how **Mr.URUKUMU** was drawn by an outsider, completely alien to his history and life-ways. I hope the BIG WHY behind this story justifies or, at least, partially redeems any distortions, fabrications or reversions to stereotypes I've made in his recombinant / funhouse mirror portrait or that of his supporting cast.

In fact, Mr. URUKUMU insisted that he be called Mr. in this text, though that conventional title of respect for men in the West means nothing where he comes from. He told me he's using this low-rent honorific to grab some serious distance from the more toxic concepts and all of the cultural stereotypes contained inside this "grotesque travesty: from inception to its last pathetic fizzle down to *nada*." The Baby Rookie has no place in his world, and he "doesn't care why or how he got there, as long as his ticket is a round trip, the damage he does is entirely theatrical, and his time in country, is very short." His words, not mine.

1

"A First Contact, of Sorts"

(Drums, rattles, rasps, bird & other animal sounds in darkness.)

(Lights up on Mr. URUKUMU & a small group of Tribe Men, down stage right of a huge white wall. Mr. URUKUMU places a macaw headdress on his head. Tribe Men make a percussive murmur around him.)

(Dimmed lights, all around, then spot comes up on The Boa Woman Downstage Left. She speaks through a mic; her tones are somewhat processed.)

The Boa Woman is separated spatially from the others. She also obviously came here from somewhere else. Maybe she's an anthropologist (of the non-weaponized variety), or a petroleum engineer, or a geologist, or a surveyor, or a human rights specialist from the United Nations, or a medical aid worker, maybe even an evangelist of one stripe or another? Maybe, but I know she'd find a few of these possibilities ethically reprehensible. I think (in fact, I know) that she's part of this performance ensemble. She's got the moves and fluid presence of a spoken word artist – we'll soon see and hear that. Maybe from somewhere on the East Coast of the United States – based on her nasal vowels, guttural consonants & Uzi-like delivery. Her beat-boxer licks have got some snap; you're really gonna' like how she freestyles, and chews through her set pieces. But oddly enough, what she's saying right here also sounds like a riff on an old-school anthropological text: like an ethnographic account of some sort of ritual – a psychic breakthrough and cleansing, of sorts. And this is the shot:)

The Boa Woman
"See: How the powerful shaman URUKUMU wears his dangerous headdress of macaw feathers and infuriates Kanawana, Lord of Thunder, and the *topu* and *awampewa*, his soldiers and servants."

179

(Now there's a loud blast of furious sound, then buzzing. URUKUMU flails in the air to fend off whatever is buzzing him. Then he collapses.)

"Eventually, he is struck down for his defiance by *topu* and left "weak with fright."

(Pause. The Boa Woman raises her left arm, fingers pointing skyward in a *"hear-me-now"* mudra.)

"First, he stiffens."

(Mr. URUKUMU stiffens on the ground. Drumming stops. The Tribe Men rise up.)

"Young men carry him around the village on their shoulders, shouting to fend off attacks by the *topu*."

(The Tribe Men hoist Mr. URUKUMU onto their shoulders. They run into the audience, whooping, shouting, grimacing, hissing: all the moves you'd hope to see from any group besieged by *topu*.)

"The young men smile as they carry him for his body shines with power and his luck, so say they all, rubs off."

(They make a circuit around the space and return to their beginning point. The Tribe Men place Mr. URUKUMU exactly where he was when this all began: on his back, rigid. They hiss and shoo away *topu* with their arms to protect him.)

"Again, his luck holds."
(Pause, and The Boa Woman very visibly listens before she speaks.)
"So there, the *topu* fly away-fly far enough away. Move it-move it, scram, *topu*, so say all young men. And URUKUMU comes back from his fall, completely whole – and hopefully unbroken – from his trip through the house of the spirits, yet again."

180

(Mr. URUKUMU is still for a moment, then sits bolt upright, eyes wide, arms splayed out, also wide: for a moment he looks suspiciously like Leonardo's long-neglected version of a cosmic asterisk! He works his head & neck with his hands. He loosens up his jaw muscles.)

(The Boa Woman points at Mr. URUKUMU.)

"Look: now his mouth moves. The rest of him will catch up, soon enough"

2
"Still Fakin' the Funk"

(Mr. URUKUMU stretches, blows out a hard but mellifluous breath through his Rahsaan Roland Kirk-style nose flute to announce his arrival. He's calm as he surveys the scene around him. Then he notices The Baby Rookie, stage right and up against The Big White Wall that's right behind his own back. (Where did that come from / Who built it / WHY?) The Rookie seems to be hard at work deploying devices, making and correlating measurements, snapping the occasional recon photo. Mr. URUKUMU wanders over and sticks his nose into The Rookie's "work-space," and exhales another riff.)

(The Rookie quickly shields his data from these prying eyes with no official clearance to see. He turns his back away from Mr. URUKUMU & continues to fiddle around with his toys. It's all remote access / he doesn't need to actually to see a thing.)

(Mr. URUKUMU notices a Zoom H6 Handy Recorder among The Rookie's array of gizmos. He's seen that rig; it's what the documentarians often bring to Amazonia to capture sound for

181

their videos. On that note he strolls back into the center, a few
paces downstage from The Big White Wall.)

Mr. URUKUMU
(Looking over at The Baby Rookie, occasionally, as he speaks.
More a gesture -- or a caution - than actual direct address:) When
you sit, who has to tell you, hey buddy, right now, guess what,
you're sitting?
(Mr. URUKUMU twists his neck side-to-side.)
You just sit, that's all, unless you're some kind of doofus. The news
spreads out from your butt through your skin like sweet heat: so
hey, your body says, yes, you're sitting, yet again.

(Mr. URUKUMU rises, pauses, paces, yawns, laces up his booties
though he's not wearing any, and stop-freezes occasionally as
punctuation.)

During all those hard times – my so-called formative years as a
Behaviorist when I specialized in breaking non-consensus spells by
reverse conditioning - back then I ate almost anything – l ate and
ate, like I was possessed or something – and I almost became what I
ate. When I almost erased myself, as well, over and over: that was
nearly the end of me. It came down to nothing left but skin and
wire, beneath it a buzz of nerve ends singing, and a steady need for
heat. Then again, maybe I was just looking for a way out of the
wrong kind of rain.
(Pause.)

A whole world, there it was,
Right here embedded in my own skin
In my ears, stuck on my eyeballs.
It bloomed inside me
Like an all-the-time dream,
Like some kind of first heaven
For the well-washed first born
(Or so they say in that other world
We don't want, or belong to).

But: I-held-nothing of it, then
I was torn in two.
But: I-saw-nothing of it, then,
Now: I see a lot more, yeah,
I see a lot better, too,
I really do, don'tcha' know,
not kidding you, not a bit.

(Mr. URUKUMU puts on shades, walks over to a nearby classroom splayed out in front of the big white wall. He sits off to one side of the classroom with his back against the wall.)

(Then Mr. URUKUMU sights The Baby Rookie, yet again. This time he's set up another recon post – this bent to move things around stems from The Rookie's special training. Field recon needs to shift, frequently, to cross up any attempts by the target at possible counter-recon, or – you never know! – even a retaliatory strike. The Rookie's hard at entering GPS data into his laptop & reading inputs from his remote field weather station & motion detection sensors – which currently register movement outside his vision. He's also deployed a zoom-augmented GoPro video camera to complement his Handy Recorder to thoroughly document the coming action. For training / documentation / QA-QC purposes, only (always looking for only the highest quality examples of "a good colonial education" process), as well as later analysis by other specialists.)

(Mr. URUKUMU waves in The Baby Rookie's direction – just to let him know that he knows The Rookie's new position & to let him know that Mr. URUKUMU – as a formerly practicing Behaviorist / despite or because of all those years of operant conditioning – is still steel-trap alert & thoroughly on the case. The Baby Rookie sees his "targeted" wave but doesn't reciprocate, & covers the lens of his GoPro to confuse the issue. Mr. URUKUMU throws up his hands in a half-shrug of fake-dudgeon, but cracks a huge simultaneous smile.)

(A Teacher – dazzling, positively coruscating – dressed all in white, with white sparklers flaming from his earlobes, a big stick in one hand, leads in the group of Tribe Men. Each Tribe Man is held by a neck leash & all the leashes are looped together so the Teacher can move the whole group – like a conductor (or something much worse / something much more insidious). The Tribe Men all duck-walk in a line: they've been learning idioms in English, and here they embody "getting all your ducks in a row" for the Teacher. They stop on command: "Whoa-up, little dogies," barks the Teacher. Each Tribe Man must now rise up – convincingly – like a duck shaking water off its feathers, and give forth an equally convincing quack. Those slow to rise, or clumsy in their movements, or taking an obviously lackadaisical stab at quackery, are corrected with a sharp / abrupt jerk on the leash. They're all connected, so all are similarly affected when each Tribe Man gets his inevitable jerk. Tempers are strained. The Teacher leads the Tribe Men as they fan out in a semi-circle from the white wall.)

Mr. URUKUMU
Like I said:
For a long time
I could see nothing

(The Teacher whacks The Big White Wall with his stick near Mr. URUKUMU's ear.)

Teacher
Sssssshhhh, you dark benighted heathen varlet-skanks. First, you must listen to me.

Mr. URUKUMU
Now that was my first big mistake. Now I - (... **Teacher whacks URUKUMU with his big stick ...**) see better ... OW! Fuck!!

184

(The Teachers unrolls a list of words from the top of the white wall. The list includes: déclassé, psychical, zoophile, epigraphist, facetious, and shillelagh. The Teacher tugs on the master-control leash and a Tribe Man / (aka "His True Star") rises up. Convincingly. Teacher points to *déclassé & psychical*; the Tribe Man ("His True Star") says each word, convincingly. The Teacher gives his Star an "atta'-boy" & the Star goes back to his starting point. The Teacher tugs on the leash again and another Tribe Man – this one's aka, "His Other Star" – rises up, equally convincingly, and does a fine job with *zoophile & epigraphist* in the finest of (very actorly) Mid-Atlantic accents. Another "atta'-boy" for another "Star" & yet another feather in the Teacher's "war bonnet" of cognitive conquests. The Teachers strokes both Stars & encourages them to stroke each other – which they do. All the other Tribe Men stumble when it's their turn – either by not ginning up convincing physicality or mangling the Mid-Atlantic nuances of *facetious & shillelagh*. The Teacher tugs hard / abruptly on the master-control leash after each misstep. This jerks the whole group & tempers are close to boiling. The last Tribe Man / aka "His Fucking Dummy" must be dragged to the white wall by the control leash, but the Teacher can't make him say shillelagh or talk, at all. The Teacher smacks him repeatedly with his stick but still, no dice. The Teacher forces aka "His Fucking Dummy's" head down to the floor with the master-control leash – irritating all the others.

Teacher
(Points to "His True Star.")
Can you tell me how to say this word?

("His True Star" rises, quite convincingly, from the disheveled / angry pile of ducks, but "His Other Star" rises, also, and grabs "His True Star" by the neck, throws him back & steps to the front to dispositively declaim:)

His Other Star

Shillelagh, shillelagh ...

(Pause. "His Other Star" turns to "His True Star" & jeers like in a jump-rope chant:)

Shillelagh ... Shillelagh ... shillelagh ... shillelagh ...

("His True Star" grabs "His Other Star" mid-word, by the neck:)

Shillelagh ... shille – Aaack!

(They scuffle, punch, kick, spout loud glossolalic nonsense at each other.)

Teacher

You're doing well.

(The Teacher whacks The Big White Wall next to Mr. URUKUMU's head. URUKUMU jumps up – pretty convincingly for a mere kibitzer - & moves quickly away from the whole semi-circular fiasco. The two "Stars" push each other one more time then sit.)

You're both doing so very well.

(The Teacher shakes the leash attached to "His Fucking Dummy" again , abruptly / violently, again increasing the group's overall irritation. The Teacher admonishes "His Fucking Dummy":)

You ... you fucking dummy ... you need to watch, listen, and do.

(The Teacher jerks "His Fucking Dummy" up on his feet – forget about the convincing duck act this time around.)

Watch ... listen ... do. All of you, now ...

(The Teacher conducts the group with his stick.)

Entire Tribe Man Student Group
(With exception of "His Fucking Dummy.")
Watch ... listen ... do – do –do.

(The Teacher jerks "His Fucking Dummy's" face around to watch the Teacher's lips.)

Shillelagh ... Shil - le – lagh. I'll say it one more time: very slow & very loud:

(The Teacher screams:)
Shillelagh!!!
(Pause. The Teacher holds "His Fucking Dummy's" chin in a death grip & says into the "Dummy's" face:)
You gotta' watch ... you really gotta' listen ... then it's time for you to do – to do – to do.
(The Teacher conducts the group with his stick.)
... do ... do ... do ...

Entire Tribe Man Student Body
(With the exception of "His Fucking Dummy")
Do – do – do – do – do – do ... (Group continues the do-do-do low drone volume until the Teacher smacks The Big White Wall.)

("His Fucking Dummy" can't really talk because the Teacher's grasp on his chin is too tight. He shakes his head, makes painful, non-intelligible noises. One giant tear barely rolls down his cheek. One side of his mouth forms a grimace.)

(The Teacher manipulates "His Fucking Dummy's" mouth & jaw while he pronounces the word shillelagh.)

Teacher
Shillelagh ... shillelagh ... shillelagh ... shillelagh ... shillel ... fuck it all.
(Teacher smacks The Big White Wall again. The group chorus stops.)
Just shillelagh. Nothing-but-shillelagh.
(Pause.)
The Teacher moves his hand back and forth in front of "His Fucking Dummy" who never blinks, or reacts in any way.)
Nothing.   But.   Shillelagh.
(The Teacher sighs. Taps "His Fucking Dummy's" skull with his fist.)
Do you live inside here, somewhere? Is all this like a dream to you? Do you even exist?

187

(The Teacher abruptly jerks "His Fucking Dummy" off to one side of the white wall. The Teacher barks in his best doggie-training command voice:)
Stay over there.
(The Teacher tugs hard on the master-control leash. More grumbling among the Tribe Men students.)
Up, up, all of you ... up now! Place your backs against The Big White Wall for a tongue check. That's the ticket. It's time for a tongue check.

(Tribe Men student body lines up against The Big White Wall, facing the audience. URUKUMU quietly comes closer. The Baby Rookie carefully documents this extraordinarily polished display of pedagogical technique.)

Mr. URUKUMU
Like I said about all of this shillelagh shit – that was my first big mistake?

(The Teacher hits the wall near URUKUMU again with his stick & URUKUMU jumps.)

Damn, Jim! Cut the crap, already!

Teacher
(Ignores URUKUMU.) Open your mouths! All of you. Stick out your worthless / ugly / inept / totally-thoroughly crapulent tongues. Say *aaaaaahhhh!* Really loud, this time.

(The entire Tribe Men student body sticks out tongues, simultaneously. Everyone says *aaaaaahhhh!* with different tonal colors and the drone they make holds steady while the Teacher walks the line and inspects their tongues with care.)

Ok. That's better, that one's almost the right size ... almost.
(The Teacher stops to look at one tongue in greater detail.)

... that one ... yes, that's a much better texture. About time, I say.
(Pause to study that beautifully textured tongue.)
Now. Everyone. Bite down hard on those totally-thoroughly
crapulent tongues. **(The Teacher conducts with his stick:)**
Do ... do ... do ... do .... do ...

**(Tribe Men bite into their tongues and make a chorus of
individual riffs on their personal pain. As usual, "His True Star" &
"His Other Star" compete to do the most self-damage, to cause
themselves the most self-inflicted trauma. The rest of the Tribe
Men Student Body is convincingly more restrained about it.
However, "His Fucking Dummy" is merely fakin' the funk – as is
his wont to do in these kinds of situations.)**

**(The Teacher continues his "do ... do ... do ... do mantra"
throughout this bite-down exercise.)**

**(Mr. Urukumu walks center stage. He stops & looks into his
cupped palms.)**

**(Lights go down slowly on the "classroom." In fading light, the
Tribe Men ditch their leashes, grab the Teacher, & twist their
leashes around his extremities & neck – with one Tribe Man on
each arm and leg, another on his head / neck - & pull forcefully.
The Teacher continues his "Do ... do ... do encouragement until his
neck snaps, & it all sounds like this: Do ... do ... do ... do ...
Aaaaaccckkk! Snap!)**

**(A single spot goes up slowly on Mr. URUKUMU as chaos rules
the classroom.)**

Mr. URUKUMU
Like I said: that first time,
Way back when I was a Behaviorist,
That first time, I held nothing I could ever really see:

189

Zed, zilch, zero, nada, bupkis, even
And I'm just saying what I was not seeing:
Flat - Freakin' - Nothing
But now, I can see a whole lot better

(Mr. URUKUMU holds up his hand – palms out.)

Right now, there's a world,
Right here in my skin
And it's a whack-whack-world,
it's so dope, it's so bomb as shit: it's so goddamn terminally /
interminably hip –
(And where do I keep getting these words from?
They're not mine, no way, never were.)
But you can see it too, now. No?
Can't you?
(Pause.)
All of this stuff before and I saw nothing
Like nothing-nothing kept on looping
Through this same dream, just nothing
Like the one I kept on – kept on having, see:
I'd lay me down, then my head drops, way down on the floor,
Straight out the bottom of my brain.
I'd go to sleep, and always, it's that same-same
bopped up dream, again.
I sure am glad, now, that I don't see that kind of nothing, no more
I sure am glad, now, that kind of nothing stopped.

**(A big crash from the classroom. Sounds of objects bouncing off
the white wall, glass breaking, laughter, & the Tribe Men Student
Body surges past Mr. URUKUMU towards down-stage right.
They hang out in a group laughing, poking at each other in play,
telling jokes.)**

**("His Fucking Dummy" comes out last, by himself. He's not
laughing; he doesn't join the group. His mood seems to be a**

190

critical side-effect of the group gestalt. There's blood on his hands, on his body, on his clothes. He stands opposite the group and throws Mr. URUKUMU a critical side-eye & a half-sneer.)

(Mr. URUKUMU just shrugs at "His Fucking Dummy.")

Who knows?
A dream like that one could grow feet, and some pretty sharp claws
A dream like that might escape, and become a big-old story
Or some kind of rogue mongo of a screamer-dream
With its own crazy-righteous agenda.
No?

("His Fucking Dummy" responds to Mr. URUKUMU's shrug by holding up a placard with this message: *"At the level of individuals, violence is a cleansing force."* [1] Mr. URUKUMU registers that message with a short salute.)

I hear you, Brother, I get
Your drift, you're not like
all the rest, but you're not the first, too.
It will feel ... it does feel, so good,
To crush the neck of he who messed
With you the worst with your heel
But while you glory in the struggle
You be sure to keep one eye peeled
For a dark sign in the sky
And when that old-man Reaper Drone
Buzzes low over your head, it's time
For you to fly, its time
To creep and to hide, my Brother
You can't fight another day
If you're dead, and they won't stop
'Til they've fed you to the forest

191

3
"How I Hurt Myself"

(Lights up on Mr. URUKUMU & Baby Rookie Downstage Center.
Mr. URUKUMU sits, gagged & tied to a chair. Baby Rookie walks
around him in a circle. Think: a much less self-possessed Vic Vega-
Wannabee / Mr. Blonde circling / torturing a captured cop in
Reservoir Dogs – minus the physically demonstrative violence.
Baby Rookie totes a scruffy-snubby old-school M16 & eats wieners
compulsively while he talks, barks, howls or whispers at Mr.
URUKUMU. Baby Rookie also uses these wieners to punctuate,
conduct and emphasize various points in his story. Baby Rookie
chomps, burps, wipes his mouth & chin with his arm, & dribbles
meat as he holds forth.)

Baby Rookie
(Eats. Talks, paces, circles, bobs & weaves, & menaces Mr.
URUKUMU with the wiener.)
… it was 5th grade … (Baby Rookie scratches his head with the
wiener) … yeah, it was 5th, I was still in middle school, ya' know ….
last year in Middle School, just before I started Junior High …
(Stops) … hey, dude, did you like Junior High?
(Pause. Baby Rookie prods Mr. URUKUMU with a wiener.)
Well fuck me hard, I clean forgot. You don't talk our language, you
don't got no money, and now I'm thinking, you ain't got no culture,
neither. You never got civilized did'ja? You are one lucky mother,
huh?
(Pause to burp, chomp, and pace a bit.)
Tell you what: I hated school from the jump, especially Junior High.
All that time, teachers fucking with my head, you know? That's
what school's all about. Especially Junior High. It's their last best
chance to put the big freeze on your brain and your balls. Teach
you how to fuck yourself, and whistle Dixie, too. Can you dig it?
(Pause.) I mean: Can You Dig It? (Baby Rookie punctuates his
question with the wiener. Pause.)

Silly Robot. I forgot again. You've never been formally tuned and tempered. You ain't nothing but a sane-eyed savage ... just metabolizing, nothing more than ... but still evolving ... there's still hope. Maybe some day, more and more so, you'll be a real human being ... just like me.

(Baby Rookie makes a rapier sharp flourish in the air close to Mr. URUKUMU's head with the wiener.)

Anyway, I'm in 5th grade, and I stay home – wishing I was stoned and I'm so bored so I watch a re-run of a real war, an old war, somewhere in the Falkland Islands – wherever that is - you know, an old school real-time news-really kind of video, on my TV, just for lil' ol' me.

(Pause to beam with pride of remembrance.)

Pretty radical concept, don'tcha' think? Big lush fake leather chair, a gi-normous Mountain Dew, and Nacho Cheese Doritos, right next to my elbow, one hand in my pants and both eyes glued to this afternoon's Big Movie – only this movie was the real thing once ... for these guys in the frame, anyway. Real blood, real gore, real certified kills, all that cool pyrotechnic stuff, and shit. You know what I'm sayin'?

(Pause. Prods, then bops Mr. URUKUMU on the head with a fresh wiener.)

Doink-Doink-Doink ... that's right ... you don't know from TV, either-neither.
What a dweeb!

(Pause. Baby Rookie expels huge breath + chunks of half-chewed wiener at Mr. URUKUMU.)

Anyway ... where was I? Oh yeah, I fake sick, yet again – my Mama-san never could tell the difference, what a stoned out tank of gas she was – and I'm watching this replay of the re-run. They showed it over five fuckin' times how this French-made Argentine-fired Exocet missile – really old tech, now – plows straight into the HMS Sheffield, and just blows the living shit out of it. I mean, precisely. I mean right on the fuckin' money.

(Baby Rookie tickles Mr. URUKUMU's chin with the wiener.)

193

You know, true precision is such an awesome rush. Don't you think?

(Pause. Baby Rookie holds Mr. URUKUMU's head and knock-knock-knocks on his noggin with the wiener.)

Anybody home. Anything happenin' in there.

(Baby Rookie drops Mr. URUKUMU's chin.)

Lost in your dream-time again, huh? Like an old zoo-lion in a zoo-cage, huh? You guys just doin' it, steady doin' it, but you never really BE nothing, do you? Huh?

(Baby Rookie shrugs, shakes his head.)

Sounds like some kind of plan, I guess.

(Invasive Surround Audio soundtrack intrudes, here. This really confuses Baby Rookie & it shows. It confused me, too, the first time I heard it and I still don't know the meaning, intentions, or motivations of the talk-talk behind this barb-fest. Or the true source of the voices, either. Though I think – if you listen closely to the caterwaul of goading, taunting, cloying, baiting (sometimes, outright hazing) embodied in the stream of ghost-babble (but all of it, babble with an alleged higher purpose, however recondite) you'll probably see this whole spiel as a, mostly overt, ruse to get a rise out of The Baby Rookie, to evoke anger / frustration / despair, bordering on hysteria. To torment the apprentice torturer with an intimate, but also wide-angle view of his own limits, design flaws, personal paranoia-scapes and failures to fully be in and engage with the world outside his own head.)

(Mr. URUKUMU instantly recognizes this skillful application of operant techniques from his storied days as a Behaviorist. Perhaps he approves of the obvious finesse behind this verbal flogging, regardless of his estimate – viewed through the mature lens of his own deep costs for such inconsequential benefits - of the ultimate value of Behaviorism, per se. But he's not talking, so I can't say. I think the voices stem from the layers of control routines imposed over time on The Baby Rookie's developing mind / brain matrix. What Augusto Boal calls the Cops-in-Our-Heads that block, parry,

choke off and distort all our attempts to shed these masochistic shell-games, and just "break into blossom.")

(One thing, though, for sure: if Baby Rookie doesn't blow his cerebral freak-show sky-high, and light up all his tender guarded zones of unlove with something true, something better, something more devotional than another stupid curse, and real soon at that, he'll be spitting out animo links like stars-cherries-horseshoes from the mouth of a slot machine. What a mess; what a bitter fate; what a sad waste of talent. And the ball is now in his court.)

Voice 1: Killer pathology he's got going on here, no?

Voice 2: Or you might say: looks like he's fixin' to collide, and split, and liberate his own immortal ions in one bright flash.

Voice 1: Or you might say: he pumps enough gravitas to spawn his own event horizon ...

Voice 2: ... or roll heat straight uphill ...

Voice 1: ...take that: you Fascist 2nd Law of Thermodynamics ...

Voice 2: ... or you might say: his face fills our flat-screens with tears ...

Voice 1: ... bottom-of the-well tears, and teary treacle, too ...

Voice 2: ... or Hollywood Ectoplasms, tearing up, hoofing down the Ave. like way-gone Kundalini zombies...

Voice 1: ... or teary-eyed Slobs of War on promenades of kneejerk denial

Voice 2: ... or stoned-out teary-bleary-eyed blubberball grognards, reminiscin' 'bout their glory days / in Pharoah's army ...

Baby Rookie (At /): Hey! I'm into something deep, here. Would you please just shut-the-fuck-up!

Voice 1: Looks like time to walk back our expectations? No?

Voice 2: Ya' think?

(Baby Rookie holds this headache in his palms, shakes his head, looks around & shrugs it off.)

Baby Rookie

What was that funny white stuff cut with, anyway?
(Baby Rookie takes deep breaths then continues his story for Mr. URUKUMU's edification & amazement. Mr. URUKUMU appears to be sleeping.)
So the last time I saw this replay of that missile hit the cruiser ... I can still remember this like it's happening right now, dude ... the last time I noticed this one guy near the cruisers fantail ... one itty-bitty little guy ... and he's flapping his arms around like ... like he ... like he's trying to fly away, you know, like a little bird ...

(Surround Audio interrupts again:)

Voice 2: ... more blue-ice blue & super-size enormous that your own steely-blue embroidered eyes ...

Voice 1 & 2: ... soft-pretty-hot-sexy lies, strewn with heat, long and loud ...

Voice 2: ... then it's time to get you some better gods.

Voice 1: Before your claws retract, before your lights go out, before your vital spark gets eaten up by the crowd.

Baby Rookie: Hey ... do you mind? You don't belong here in my head.

Voice 2: Before you're full beset by swarms of roaming restless dead.

Voice 1: Before all the wicked sly-juice inside you just dries up, and dies.

Voice 2: Hey ... that's pretty creepy.

Baby Rookie: Sure as Hell, That's Creepy! I said: get out of my head, you fucks!

(Baby Rookie recons the room before he picks up the thread of his story. He's pretty sure at this juncture that this is not some synesthetic residue of yesterday's pathetic bacchanal.)
(To Mr. URUKUMU:)
So he flaps his arms real hard ... **(Baby Rookie demos the proper flapping technique)** ... like this ... then he falls ... o-o-o-o-ver the side ... just like that.
(Pause. Shrug of a disinterested stoic.)
Then he's gone. Just like that. **(Pause & huge breath like unloading years of pent-up false identities, and their masks. Now he can say what he feels & believes.)**
What a rush. One second he's there: he's pumping his arms, he's about to get some lift-off and fly-fly away. Then he's not. Got to say it again – precision ... precision ...
And again: PRE - CI - SION ... such an awesome rush.

(Another Surround Audio interruption creeps back up on Baby Rookie. At first he treats the enveloping sonic fog like a swarm of irritating bugs, but gradually the truth dawns: this is all about him, all about the massive gaps in his personal soul-craft, and it seems to emanate from his insides out.)

Voice 1 & 2: Hey, Brother! Hey. Rookie! Hey Baby-Baby! It's *Time To Straighten Up and Fly Right!*

Baby Rookie: The hell you say!

Voice 1: No, you're supposed to say: *you're chokin' me, you're chokin' me …*

Voice 2: *… loose your hold & I'll set you free …*

Baby Rookie: What the Fuck! Can't you get it through your skulls what I'm up to here?

Voices 1 & 2: No, no, no, stop doin' the do! You gotta' *cool down papa, don't you blow your top!*

Baby Rookie: And I'm saying: Shut the Fuck Up!! Can't you see I'm interrogating this prisoner. Pretty soon, it's gonna' get enhanced!

Voice 1: Well, you're not you know. Not really.

Voice 2: Technically speaking, this lame attempt at interrogation is really a load of crap. Technically … it's – what's the term of art, here?

Voice 1: Piss-poor, maybe? *Muy stupido, tal vez?*

Voice 2: How 'bout *Abgefuckt total?*

Voice 1: Fact is, your whole interrogation is more like poorly executed self-flagellation.

Voice 2: So would you like your flagellation also self-enhanced?

Baby Rookie: This is not too freaking helpful, you know. I'm trying to do a job on this guy. I'm trying to get this right.

Voice 1: Rookie, O-Rookie, my Baby-Baby Rookie: none of this matters for you.

Voice 2: We happen to know that – at 1437 hours, this very day – you're gonna' freeze up on The Big White Wall.

Voice 1: You're gonna' dingle-dangle through the jingle-jangle afternoon. Nothing else you can do.

Voice 2: You're gonna' twist back and forth in the hot-hot breeze.

Baby Rookie: Again, I say, the Hell You Say! **(Pause.)** So how do you know that anyway?

Voice 1: We've got some real Intel. Way better than what you've got to go on.

Voice 2: We see way more and you don't see nothin'.

Voice 1: It goes like this, Rookie, pay attention to me. A wise guy once said: "the less you see ....

Voice 2: ... the less you know ...

Voice 1: ... and the less you know ...

Voice 2: ... the easier ... you breathe.

Voice 1: So grab you a few quick easy breaths, Baby Rookie.

Voice 2: Cuz' you don't know nothin' yet.

Voice 1: Cuz' you're kinda' just a cut-out. A mope, and low-down too. Just some kinda' usual mook. Nothing but a chump-change schlub, don'tcha' know.

Voice 2: Cuz' you ain't nothin' ... but - A - Green - Ass - Rookie.

(Baby Rookie seems paralyzed by his dawning awareness that his wicked agency is compromised, or possibly just a major delusion from the get-go. He shambles like a dumb-struck June Bug through the space – bereft of mission / robbed of meaning / rudderless & spiraling down the drain of all his former identities. He passes - in oblivion – close by Mr. URUKUMU who sticks his foot out & trips him. He hits the floorboards with a mighty thud & appears to stay down for the count.)

Voice 1: Don't let all this turn you 'round, Baby Rookie. Just pop your lid on, take up your body and assume your position behind that Big White Wall.

Voice 2: It's time to shoot on through that solid gloom you're wearing like a shroud.

Voice 1: Blast your soul and body rockets full-bore! Be big, be loud!

Voice 2: Or don't. Just don't forget that lid. No employee gets a pass on wearing their official lid.

Voice 1 & 2: And you are just another Em - Ploy - Yee. See?

(Baby Rookie does as instructed. He pops on his Smurf hat and shuffles – I suppose listless & distracted, possibly also thoroughly demoralized, might best describe the arc & wobble of his shuffle – over to The Big White Wall and disappears behind it.)

4
"Meet My Signature Wound"

"The human mind was not made for war.
That's the starting point for everything."

General George Casey (former Commanding General,
Multi-National Force / IRAQ   2004-2007

(Lights up on the Big White Wall. Spot shines on the top of it.
URUKUMU sits with his back to the wall in the right corner.
Black Ops Troopers in standard issue desert *camo* line up in a tight
squad formation, down stage left. Each Trooper's head is wrapped
in a tight, black do-rag. They wear combat face paint, wide-
receiver gloves, and carry M4A1 carbines with ammo. An
occasional M26 accessory shotgun system may be found scattered
among the group. The Black Ops Squad Leader packs a long-
barreled .51 MM SCAR-H & a Heckler & Koch .45 sidearm. A
football helmet – specially engineered to dampen concussive
shocks - is slung over each Trooper's back like a bandolier.)

So who are these people? What forces, bold plans and desires brought them
together? What's the source of their dubious esprit de corps? Who do they
actually work for? Where does all the money come from to dress, arm and
provision these cadres of Neo-Praetorian Guards, all strapped and
hormonally swollen with gung-ho / can do.

Where did they get these sophisticated heaters, this state-of-the-art
ammunition, this lethal level of training? Their tactics are blunt and clear
enough, but what are their strategies, their final goals? When they're
finished, if ever, who ascends / who crashes down and rots. Which Big
Who corners all the black chips; and which little Who's lose their asses?

Are they Our Own Right Now's version of the ancient Dream Police?
(Expendable / Regenerative) Appendages of the latest Big Bad Who? Are

they, even, of this here earth at all? Whose dreams do they preserve,
protect, project into the world's steady throb? And whose dreams are they
deputized to deface, distort, destroy, and lob – with no ceremony – into
the pit?

From where and when did this evil creep from into our world? Through
what door, down which road, by water, on wings, never quiet but hidden
in the dust kicked up by boots after boots after boots? Where does it
gestate and hover – on tap / on call –until it's brought forth into real
presence like a destroying genie or an angel of menace and decay? Does it
ever really sleep? Why does it never stop?

A touch of skin on skin, or a cool wind off the sea won't / can't / never
ease our fever. Why do we do this to us?

**(Throughout the coming rappel sequence, Mr. URUKUMU plays
objective (more or less scientific) observer, fascinated bystander,
or editorializes with partisan zeal using his body and actions for
show & tell. Occasionally he scootches closer – sliding on his butt
– or gets up and walks around. Sometimes, he even tries to
interfere. The Black Ops Troopers react both predictably, and in
novel ways. It's totally up to them in each moment how they deal
with – or ignore – Mr. URUKUMU. There's no script for his
intentions or their interactions during this part: let's just let the
uncertainty ride & see what happens!)**

**(Black Ops Squad Leader takes position down stage center from
The Big White Wall. He sets up a tripod and spyglass, sights in &
then fiddles around with fine-tuning the instrument. A Lance
Corporal (or a Gunny) sets out a wire basket full of footballs
behind him and assumes an *at-ease* position. (His main job is to
keep the flow of footballs going for the Squad Leader during this
drill). The Squad Leader blows his whistle & the squad of Black
Ops Troopers begins to run in place all chanting *hup-hup-hup!* He
blows whistle again & the Back Ops Troopers *hup-hup-hup!*
forward at a trot and disappear behind The Big White Wall. Black**

Ops Squad Leader blows whistle yet again & a rope (rappelling line) is thrown over the wall.)

(The Black Ops Troopers move through their rappel work in the following sequence: 1) as the Troopers appear (singly) at top of The Big White Wall, they lock into position on the rappel line with their carabiner systems, strap on their football helmet, and wait for the signal from The Squad Leader. 2) The Squad Leader blows whistle, and begins *hup-hup-hup* chant; Troopers on rappel make jerky descent in time to their Squad Leader's *hup-hup-hup!* 3) The Squad Leader lobs footballs close to Trooper's head as they each descend: each football flashes & makes an explosive sound when they hit the wall. Like a concussion grenade to weakly simulate the shock of shoulder launched rockets or nearby IED's. (Conditioning for the future, a test of nerve, or will, or all of that?) 4) As the Troopers reach the floor, they unhook from the line, remove and stow their football helmets and quick trot to (alternately) one side or the other of the Squad Leader, and assume the at-ease position. 5) As each Trooper falls in-line, the Black Ops Squad Leader blows his whistle for the next Trooper to advance down The Big White Wall. 6) As the drill proceeds, an assistant, a Lance Corporal, (or a Gunny), steadily refills the Squad Leader's supply of concussive footballs.)

(Finally, a last Black Ops Trooper we will call, again – The Baby Rookie – appears at the top of The Big White Wall. He has a full complement of armaments (but was issued that same scabby/shabby old-school M16), and combat accoutrements, the whole desert *camo* drag, but no do-rag / no football helmet combo. Instead, The Baby Rookie wears that same purple Smurf hat. He also wears a retro Captain Midnight Secret Decoder Ring – but with no instructions for deploying said arcane device. He hooks into the line, begins his advance downward, then freezes - *mid-hup!* – on the wall. All the others *hup-hup-hup*, now, with the Squad Leader lobbing flash/concussive passes, but The Baby Rookie does not react. They all *hup-hup-hup!* again but The Baby Rookie just cringes/cowers, dangles & twists – just like the term, *twists in the wind*, would suggest. The Black Ops Squad Leader steps away from his observation post, marches over to the Big White Wall, blows his whistle forcefully & long, & barks out a staccato steam of *hups!*, very distinctly. The Baby Rookie continues to dangle & twist.)

(The Black Ops Squad Leader returns to his post, blows his whistle again, & all the Troopers slap on their football helmets & perform 2 on 1 blocking drills beneath the dangling/twisting Baby Rookie. The Black Ops Squad Leader blows his whistle again – 3 sharp blasts – and 2 of the Troopers begin to push The Baby Rookie back & forth like a pendulum while a 3rd - a Lance Corporal (or Gunny) - fires hard passes – solid as a stretched rope – straight at The Baby Rookie as he swings. The 3 Troopers involved in this maneuver *hup-hup-hup!* in unison as they work. Each time the football hits The Baby Rookie (with a flash/concussive impact), he groans as he absorbs these blows & the Squad Leader yells *Oorah, Booyah, Hooyah, Hooah,* or some variation on that celebrated man-bond growl of approval. When the Trooper throwing passes, misses, the Black Ops Squad Leader head butts his helmet.)

(The Black Ops Squad Leader returns to his post, blows his whistle, & the Black Ops Troopers return to their line and assume at-ease positions. The Squad Leader leaves his post and marches up to the dangling Baby Rookie. He slowly turns him upside down on rope. The Squad Leader slowly removes his own do-rag, then caresses The Baby Rookie's cheeks & kisses him long, hard & deep on the lips (& more so). Then the Squad Leader removes The Baby Rookie's Smurf hat, takes The Rookie's KA-BAR from its sheath & - very tenderly – cuts his throat.)

Here, The Baby Rookie shares the same fate as Jerzy Kosinski's character, Ludmilla, in "The Painted Bird." Once again, an odd duck, as identified by the (squad, crewe, gang, community, collective?) becomes the dead duck to atone for its Otherness. I been told we're not supposed to worship &

adore this book, anymore. But when Stellan Skarsgaard, a major actor in the film version, says: "Though this film takes place during the Second World War, the same things, the same horrors happen today. We need to remember what war is and to learn from it," I can hardly disagree.

(The Black Ops Squad Leader tastes The Baby Rookie's blood, smears some on his own face, takes a handful more and makes his handprint on the Big White Wall. The Squad Leader blows his whistle & the other Troopers do the same-so, one at a time – like a solemn ritual – with various degrees of enthusiasm, reluctance, hesitation. The last Trooper in line doesn't step up to do it. The Squad Leader blows his whistle again, but still the last Trooper doesn't move. The Squad Leader jerks his head & two other Troopers grab the last man, force his hand into the blood, then onto his lips, his cheeks, & then force his full hand onto the white wall to leave his handprint. The two Troopers return to the main line, flanking the Squad Leader. The Trooper forced to share The Baby Rookie's blood stands alone for a long moment, seemingly staring into space. Then he walks over to The Baby Rookie's dangling body, cuts him down, rubs The Baby Rookie's hand in the blood from The Rookie's own neck wound, & drags him over to the wall to make the Squad's last print.)

Movies about the raw brutality – and shared complicity – of war, its obscene crimes & the grinding toll on combatants and civilians, are legion. After Vietnam and, now, following a succession of more current wars, the special problems of soldiers returning / readjusting to civilian life – and whatever passes for civilized civilian behavior in their home locales – after their tour(s) claimed a major share of Hollywood's focus. "The Hurt Locker," "The Deer Hunter," "American Sniper," "First Blood," "Platoon," "Coming Home," "Born on the 4th of July," "Billy Lynn's Long Halftime Walk," and many more explore this grim / familiar master-narrative for the uninitiated. Many former soldiers I know claim they've never watched anything in this vein.

And in all of this great "band of brothers" chain of movie being, "Da 5 Bloods" is a being of another order.

But "A Few Good Men" & "In the Valley of Elah" focus more directly on the unofficial / unwritten code of Omertà that maintains silence and distributes complicity among perpetrators of what could be termed, war crimes. Or egregious breaches of law or protocol during "peace-time" routines that result in some level of carnage, extreme abuse, even death. Like the police: remember what happened to Serpico when he was too clean for dirty cops to trust? Or what about the decades of "enhanced interrogation" practiced by the Burge crew of Chicago PD officers? Or that notorious on-the-hush collaboration between the same Chicago red squad cops & the government's COINTELPRO FBI minions in the assassination of Black Panther Party leaders, Fred Hampton & Mark Clark. Or the CIA's Project MKUltra mind control experiments. Or Operation "Fearless Johnny." Or the Philadelphia PD's C4 incendiary attack on MOVE - while the Police Commissioner, Gregore Sambor sings (in so many words) "We don't need water, let the mother-fucker burn." And there's so much more.[1]

Or more currently, what made those other officers of the Minneapolis PD turn their backs / avert their faces / refuse to engage / or actively assist and actually enable murder – right there on Main Street! – while Derek Chauvin squeezed breath & life out of George Floyd with his knee / boot / and poisonous venom. While people in the crowd around the murder scene implored Chauvin and the others to let this man breathe? Are they just that racist at the core? Is this Omertà in action again: great unity among the "brothers-in-arms" performed to daunt and intimidate, for all those public eyes to drink in, and be forewarned? Or all of this, and more?

So now it looks like The Baby Rookie's staked his own claim to a small corner in the Valley of Elah. At least, symbolically. His inability to fall-in-line & just do what had to be done, or accept necessary discipline and redeem himself, later, made his very existence a rebuke to his comrades. And rebuke begets derision begets violent "Painted Bird" retribution from the faithful in the squad. Or so it goes "In the Valley of Elah."

(The Black Ops Squad Leader blows his whistle, again, & the Troopers strip The Baby Rookie down to his *camo* diaper. They stack their weapons on top of his body, throw his standard desert *camo* on top of the stack & wait with their heads down. The Squad Leader blows his whistle & the entire Black Ops Squad evaporates.)

By now, Mr. URUKUMU is tired of kibitzing this silly ritual. Silly, at least, from his point-of-view. All this stress and blood and strife: and nothing much happened, did it?. Nothing, at least, sufficient to disrupt the drift of this moment in history toward oblivion – or worse yet, repetition. All of these guys are trapped in a collective delusion and his time as a Behaviorist helped him realize that delusions like this one are like stepping on the pressure detonator of a land-mine – one rigged to explode when the pressure is released – or being trapped with rowdy drunks in a clunky beater of a car – but fake-tricked out like a Cobra to explode down the open road with no functional brakes to speak of and an unreliable driver/narrator – going way too fast-fast-fast. Such a waste of time and raw talent. When there's so much real work to be done.

(Mr. URUKUMU walks over to wall, sniffs it, tastes it, places his palms over the prints, & gets a little blood on his own palms. He sniffs the blood, tastes it, smears a little on his own cheeks. Mr. URUKUMU glides slowly over to The Baby Rookie. Peeks under the clothing, under the war gear, prods The Baby Rookie with his toe, tastes the blood again gets himself a palm-full & puts his own print on the wall with the others. Mr. URUKUMU squats near The Baby Rookie's face, & strokes him as if he were a baby in the nursery, again, and speaks to him. But this is not a baby talking baby-talk.)

Mr. URUKUMU
I'm pretty sure I saw you before this ... in my new improved dream – the very dream I've got to become to get this stuff to make some sense. When I was a Behaviorist, it all made easy sense but ... Jeez

Louise, it was all a fake!! I look around now and all I can think or say is *What The Fuck Was I Thinking?*
(Pause. Mr. URUKUMU strokes The Baby Rookie's face, again. I'd say with some desperation, but that's really not his style.)
Tell me your name. Do you know your name? Do you know who you are? Tell me ... who are you, really?

(Spotlight up abruptly on The Boa Woman, now, as our blues-inflected chanteuse. I think, maybe, this song is a response to Mr. URUKUMU's question:)

You know, Mr. URUKUMU really loves the Ur-version of this song, the best – a taste of Muddy Waters, Son House, Fred McDowell, etc. & the Delta which he's never actually seen / and maybe couldn't pin precisely on a map. But these blues came into him in some other dream, in another life, once, and inhabited his body. Back then, it felt right at home for him to be possessed and transported suchly as those Coke bottle slide sounds filled up his ears, those claw hammer fingers buzz-twitched back and forth across his own neck, it seemed. And then, all that sad-sad - exultant – transfigurational - fullness.

(Mr. URUKUMU walks over to The Boa Woman and comps with his blues-kazoo while Boa Woman sings. The Baby Rookie remains immobile during much of the song. The lights go down so slow on Mr. URUKUMU, The Boa Woman & The Baby Rookie. In terms of style, think: McKinley Morganfield aka "Muddy Waters" doing his eponymous *I'm a Man / Mannish Boy*. Only this is, more or less, a woman's take on that mythology.)

The Boa Woman

"Who I Am"
I'm a man
That's my ride
I'm a man
Can't try to hide

208

Tell my story
From the outside, in
Don't cop to passion
Got to save my own skin

I'm a man
Hu-man animal
I'm a man
Hu-man bone
I'm a man
Just want to breathe right
I'm a man
Man alone

I'm a man
Can't hang no real sun
Fever you / me always
Panic run
Hot jumpin' bones
Gotta' help me out
Spin my red-eyes wide open
'Cuz I'm all about

(The Baby Rookie stirs, raises himself up – convincingly – and
begins his slow crawl over to the Boa Woman. Maybe Mr.
URUKUMU comes over to him to serenade him personally with
some frantic blue styling's on his old kazoo. Maybe not?)

Bein' a man
Hu-man appetite
I'm a man
Hu-man fate
I'm a man
Don't want no simple light
I'm a man
Born too late

209

I'm a man
Dig me a big ol' hole
Throw in my hands & tongue
Cover up my own soul
Too much scufflin', now
'Gainst my own skin
Too far gone to say
I still got it pinned

Cuz' I'm a man
Hu-man wilderness
I'm a man
Hu-man clown
I'm a man
No-no innocence
So say how down we get to when
We get down

(The Boa Woman hands mic to The Baby Rookie. She props him up so that he can solo on the next part – it's sort of like a bridge. Think: Bob Dylan's *"I'm Pledging My Time."*)

The Baby Rookie
Ya' know I want to wear it
That starry crown
Lookin' everywhere for it
But it ain't nowhere to be found

(Now Boa Woman & URUKUMU join in singing with The Baby Rookie. And it's back to that *Mannish Boy*.)

210

All Three As Chorus
So just say how down we get to when
We get down
We get down
We get down
We get down

(Lights to black.)

Mr. URUKUMU
(From the center of the blackness;)
Right then
Old man night poured down thick sleep
Upon our lids, all a'flutter,
Bringin' on that pain face for all us kids,
Ain't no cookies, no way, ain't no jam and peanut butter,
For spooky little baby Jackie Horner
Just whispers-whispers-whispers over in a freaky corner -
And in our heads, a dark-dark mutter -
Bringin' down all the scary stories.
Before the lights go out with a big ol' crack
And our big leak star-ward just begins,
Now Ol' Big Daddy Who's parked there, too,
With a big ol' smack just for you and you,
Right there in our very own doorway.

5
"Rock My Baby All Night Long"

(Lights up on a still dim nursery. Smurf & Barney, Sesame Street, My Little Pony & Mr. Rogers, disembodied Hello-Kitties: whole pantheons of once and future characters for kiddos hang as banners, on tripods and over The Big White Wall. Babies sleep around the nursery in various spots.)

211

And so it comes to pass: The Boa Woman mutates into the Boogie Lady. We didn't know the Boa Woman possessed powers to transmogrify, to shift appearances, motives and intentions. But, apparently, she does. And we can't be certain her agenda is still relatively benevolent, didactic, disinterested, or even, maybe, strongly biased now and guided by a darker purpose. Some say, The Boogie Lady is her alter-ego, her evil-twin, her eternally persistent wound, never healing, always aching, never far enough from the surface to forget or deny. Some folks say, she's La Lucheza, personified, and we need to keep her far away from children. Really, though, she's just an actor in this old-school morality drama of Everyman as Every Baby Rookie. Or vice-versa. And as an actor, her own life with all its apogees and low-down scars is gonna' bleed right through and into the role. This is as it should be: that's the hard-won spiritual aspect of the actor's soul-craft. She doesn't just pull her characters and moves whole cloth from the nearest Skinner Box. You think?

(A shrouded Boogie Lady – in case we forget, she's The Boa Woman's main performance aka – glides through the nursery like a cat, a'hunting. She approaches each sleeping Baby and sniffs the air a few times, but never stops to disturb them. Babies show some agitation / maybe even distress as she passes, but they don't wake up. All throughout this glide process, Mr. URUKUMU comps erratically on his jaw harp & interjects the Boogie Lady's signature chant when appropriate:)

Mr. URUKUMU
The Boogie Lady's back hangin' out on the corner
The Boogie Lady's scary & the pump's broke too

(Mr. URUKUMU urges the audience to chant along with him on the back-end of the Boogie Lady theme.)

Mama put a cookie in the red cookie jar
Mama put a cookie in the red cookie jar
Mama put a cookie in the red cookie jar

212

(Mr. URUKUMU strolls into the nursery & strips away the shroud from the Boogie Lady (aka the Boa Woman). Underneath it, she is also a Baby with the same Smurf underwear as all the others – with the exception of The Baby Rookie who still wears his standard issue camo droopy-drawer didie. The Boogie Lady Baby glides to her place on the nursery floor, and sleeps. Mr. URUKUMU pats, strokes, coos at & tickles – even snorts at – all the various Babies. They react to him, but don't wake up.)

Mr. URUKUMU
(To Babies as he tickles, coos, etc.)
Now you all float nice and warm inside. Your dream goes forward and your dreams goes back-a-ways, all at the same time. Right now, you can talk to the gods, like one god talks to another. Maybe you're all gods, yourselves ... right now? Maybe for a tiny moment, now, you're all immortal?
(Mr. URUKUMU hovers over The Baby Rookie.)
Even this one.
(Mr. URUKUMU's face is very close to The Baby Rookie, now.)
You ... right now, you dream a bent dream. So how far does your dream bend, before it cracks ... (slaps his thigh) ... like that?
(Shrugs.)
At least, you'll see it better when that happens.

(Mr. URUKUMU sings the Count The Babies child-riff, *a capella*, legato, lugubriously sad – with deep sorrow & regret, like a *fado* ballad.)

"Count the Babies"
Count the Babies
Count the curves in each
Tiny mouth, count their bitty-little tongues-zez
Their lips like almonds
The upsweep-swerve of their goofy little nose-zez

Count their eyes like tiny little dots
Count and pinch and wiggle
All their piggly little toes-zez
Count 'em all, before you wake the Babies
From their own sleep in their own beauty
Count each breath they take
Count each breath they give back
Don't cry, just count
Where each breath goes-zez
Before you wake up all the Babies
Before they have so much to win
Before they learn to lose
What they know-zez

(Mr. URUKUMU sits down in the center of the nursery. Alarm clock goes off, runs down. All the Babies pop up awake. 2 Babies crawl over to The Baby Rookie and claw through the pile of stuff on top of him. These 2 Babies pull off / strew around all the standard issue desert *camo* pieces of his uniform, grab his weapons & sling them on their backs, then crawl away. All Babies are more or less constantly in motion doing something.)

(Finally, The Baby Rookie wakes up & begins to move. He flops over on all fours with difficulty like a bug-on-its-back. His crawling technique is stiffer than the others.)

(Audio: *Crazy Ragtime Bug Music.*)

(Babies in motion have the following movement / exploration sequence options:

1. Babies with weapons discharge them at random. Some shots whizz by Mr. URUKUMU, one or two may actually hit him. He laughs and bleeds; but, wounded or not, he doesn't move.

2. Babies pull around Baby Rookie's standard issue desert *camo.* They tug on it together – like a tug o' war, they pull each other around with it, tie each other up.
3. Babies knock down Smurf banners, etc. & bash them around.
4. Babies roll, tumble sideways or head over heels, beat on the floor.
5. Babies bash the alarm clock, toss it, kick it, stomp it.
6. 3 Babies group up to run 2 on 1 blocking drills (without helmets, yet!!)
7. A Baby switches on wide-screen TV which plays docu-footage from the 2nd battle for Fallujah (2004 / code name: *Phantom Fury* / in Arabic: الـفـجر - "The Dawn.")
8. Babies crawl fast or slow.
9. Babies thump on each other.
10. Babies build a tower out of the world's great religious texts – the Bible, the Koran, The Ashes of Mystery, the Bhagavad Gita, Lord of Light, Norman Vincent Peale's "Applied Theology," the Diamond Sutra, Vala, or The Four Zoas, A Low-Budget Baphomet's Guide to Subverting Paradise, The Song of Solomon, Paradise Lost, The Torah, Dianetics Made Easy, Creatures of Light & Darkness, Dark Night of the Soul, the Book of Mormon, The Song of Los, an annotated copy of The Magnificat, etc. in no particular order. They push them over / rebuild the tower / repeat the process.
11. Babies pull each other's diapers off & show each other what they got. Babies play with their own and each other's "nasty bits," as babies are so often wont to do.
12. Babies improvise.)

(A Baby accidentally shoots The Boa Woman Baby & she crumples in place. All the Babies crawl over to see. Audio stops.)

(The Baby Rookie touches The Boa Woman Baby's wound, tastes the blood, smears blood on his face, then on her face.)

(Other Babies wipe hands in blood, make handprints on the floor. 2 of the Babies crawl to the wall & make their own handprints over the Black Ops Troopers' prints.)

(Mr. URUKUMU rises and plays trembling note on his wooden flute. All the Babies stop actions, lift heads & crawl into places in a line. Mr. URUKUMU plays the original child riff in a *"trancer"* tempo & Babies follow in line as wavy crawler conga line behind as he moves across the space. Mr. URUKUMU stops at The Boa Woman Baby; all the babies make a circle around her & slow dance like sad elephants while Mr. URUKUMU plays dirge variations on the original child riff. Mr. URUKUMU changes tempo and Babies crawl off behind him, stopping at The Baby Rookie's spot. The Baby Rookie drops out, lays down on back, other babies pile stuff back on top of him. Babies follow Mr. URUKUMU behind the wall like he's the Pie-Eyed Piper.)

(The (bloody) Baby Rookie & The Boa Woman remain in place. The Boa Woman sheds her Baby clothes & slips into her (not so bloody) Boa skin while space is dark.)

(Lights down.)

6

"Several Free-Falling Worlds at Once"

(Lights up on a steaming bowl, sage burner. A large cloth for sitting, small percussion instruments, a Telecaster electric guitar blue-toothed with an off-stage amp, a small bundle of camo bush clothes, long PVC "flute" (or didgeridoo), a small wooden flute (to, eventually, be broken), a floor-level mic, down stage left.)

(A leaf pattern is projected onto the Big White Wall. A 2nd slide showing Western Brazil – the area between the *Rio Amazonas* & the *Rio Purus* is superimposed across the leaf pattern. These projections end when The Baby Rookie says: *"And we've got the heavy artillery."*)

(The Tribe Men appear. They wear distorted white masks, turtle shells, feathers, some paint. Two of them carry poles with strips of cloth & animal skulls tied to the top. Tribe Men make bird-calls, growls, wind & wing sounds: they move in a way that mimics their sounds. They interrupt these patterns at random to whirl, leap, grunt, whistle, or call out shrilly. They make other equally theatrical / only marginally realistic / very admittedly stereotypical moves.)

(Now, Mr. URUKUMU animates the *cartoon dream* he's stitched together for The Baby Rookie & a couple of the Black Ops Troopers – detached from the main assault force for greater stealth in recon & to keep a spy-eye on that possibly unreliable Baby Rookie. Mr. URUKUMU enters the space from behind the big white wall. He wears a performance costume similar to the other Tribe Men that chose a traditional approach. His face is painted red & white on opposite sides. The rest of the Tribe Men defer to him, make room, acknowledging agreed-upon performance conventions. A Tribe Man picks up the bowl & offers it to Mr. URUKUMU with much respect. He smiles, takes the bowl and drinks. The bowl contains the soul-propellant they call Honi Xuma. Then he speaks to them all:)

Mr. URUKUMU
Now, we can all become part of this here dream

(Mr. Urukumu holds up the bowl at eye level. He looks eye-to-eye & lowers the bowl. The bowl is passed one to another & all the Tribe Men drink from it. Mr. URUKUMU "sings" a low-register split tone & most of the Tribe Men flow over to spot stage right of big white wall where they create a human *Tree of Masks*. Mr. URUKUMU places the steaming bowl next to the sitting cloth, glides to wall, fits his own palm over one of the handprints, tastes his palm, & glides back to The Baby Rookie. Mr. URUKUMU stops, stirs up the air with his hands, and circuits around the prone (sleeping / unconscious?) Baby Rookie like a ratchety, nervous bird. Playing, again, to convention, he makes bird sounds as he moves. After a few circuits he stops at The Baby Rookie's head & plays an ominous, drawn-out, breathy child-riff on his wooden flute. After two more circuits, he stops at The Baby Rookie's head, again, holds The Baby Rookie's chin up to his face & speaks:)

Dream-time, Baby, it's dream time, again.
It's time to dream with your own eyes wide open, this time.
And this one's fixin' to be a stratospheric doozey, dontcha' know.

(Mr. URUKUMU gently re-releases The Baby Rookie's chin, slides over to the sitting cloth, and exhales a low, breathy tone into the mic'ed PVC flute (or didgeridoo). He holds the tone until The Baby Rookie is up on his feet.)

(The Baby Rookie wakes up into his doozey of a dream: The Baby Rookie thrashes around, knocks over the pile of stuff on top of him, startles, shows a moment of intense vertigo & leaps to his feet. He is drawn magnetically toward the *Tree of Masks* which moves its arms and legs – almost imperceptibly – while the whole *Tree* hums & buzzes at him. The Baby Rookie shows a moment of extreme fight/flight frozen terror, and then retreats quickly, finds his weapons, girds his loins, in a manner of speaking, cocks his main battle-axe and slaps his sights onto the *Tree of Masks*. He breathes deeper, more slowly, now, gets calm, lowers his weapon & flexes into wave after wave of self-assurance.)

(Finally, The Baby Rookie turns toward us, the watchers, looks down & notices his *camo* didie, shows confusion / then shame, and quickly pulls on *camo* combat pants over his baby bottoms. He

218

finds a paint stick in his pockets & paints stripes of black underneath his eyes, over his cheeks & forehead. He adjusts a black do-rag on his head. He wears no shirt to show off his ripped abs. He picks up his M4 & speaks with flat affect as if his words were being channeled or he's in the throes of a strong CNS depressant. His affect becomes more natural as this bespoke dream progresses.)

The Baby Rookie

(To Watchers and Co-Conspirators:)
Tonight, we bivouac with a war party of Kana Taxi. We've followed the spoor of our shared enemy, the Huni Kui, to this spot – between the Rio Tarauaca & the Rio Jurua.
(Pause.) Tomorrow, we're gonna' flush 'em out together. The Kana Taxi are good trackers: good eyes, ears and noses. **(The Baby Rookie pats his piece.)** And we've got the heavy artillery. And the skill to kill 'em all.

(The _Tree of Masks_ hums & buzzes louder. Mr. URUKUMU uses a rasp to enhance the texture of this subtle sound-scape. The Baby Rookie brushes the sounds away from his head, like he's brushing back a swarm of insects.)

It's a good for us that Huni Kui killed some rubber cutters 40 years back. Now, when anyone attacks work parties building new roads, or fucks up the drilling rigs, or stuffs up the new water wells with pieces of old metal junk and dead things, we can always blame it on them. We say, "See: those Huni Kui are still the same old devils" and everyone agrees. _No problemas!_ We just say, "You remember how they roll – dead tongues, dead fingers, dead dried out skulls, necklaces of dead ears strung across the forest canopy?" Hey, we say, "ya' know what: we heard these wild devils skin and eat their enemies. So whatta' ya' think a' that one?" It's one strong mojo: say it often, say it loud, say it long enough and everyone believes it.

(Pause.) Makes it easier to rub those fuckers right out if no one else cares what we do. Or how we do it.

(The *Tree of Masks* hums & buzzes louder – up and down an octave.)

(The Baby Rookie hits himself repeatedly with the flat of his hand. He opens his mouth & this weirdness inflected with no discernable affect is what comes out:)

... the dead skulls ... all the time in the world to wait ... they have ... the dead tongues ... they sing their fucked-up songs into the wind ...

(The Baby Rookie shakes his head to clear his vision, hearing, thoughts. He points his weapon all around. He finally focuses on the *Tree of Masks*, then lowers it & speaks again:)

Damn! Get the fuck out of my head! I hate that - I'm warning you. **(Pause. The Baby Rookie takes a few deep breaths to stop himself from hyperventilating. He simmers down & speaks again:)** We say that and say that and other people just help us out ... give us good intel ... ya' know, they don't like the Huni Kui either. And we get a good price to move them out of the way. Keeps a boss happy. Keeps a government happy, lots and lots of governments. Keeps Chevron happy. Texaco, too. Pfizer and Glaxo-Smith-Kline. And Novartis likes it like that. The Kana Taxi get a bounty on each one they kill. They like that, it's nice to make some real money out here in the bush. We all get all we want. Can't get any happier than that.

(2 Tribe Men leave the *Tree of Masks*, kneel down on either side of the blue cloth & ripple it like water.)

(The Boa Woman rises up as The Mother of Boas as The Baby Rookie speaks. Her rising is emergent, an unfolding into fullness. She drifts across the river like a cloud & comes to him.)

Tonight, I want The Mother of Boas all for myself. Look at that: right now she slides toward me through the forest.

(**The Boa Woman presses her body against The Baby Rookie. She extends & twines around him.**)

(**The Baby Rookie rubs & strokes The Boa Woman's skin while he speaks.**)

The Kana Taxi tell us a Boa's skin is lucky. If you rub the pattern on a Boa's skin, it's a'gonna' bring you big-loud-luck: that's what they tell us.

(**The Boa Woman becomes agitated. She takes The Baby Rookie down with her. She twines around him, slides over-off-and back onto him. Finally, she stands tense, and trembles. She turns slow, in a full circle, and flows back across the river to her point of emergence. She folds shut.**)

(**The Baby Rookie rises up stronger, stretches his body, cocks-uncocks-recocks his weapon.**)

But ya' see: I don't need luck to do what I do. I can cross all these rivers with no luck at all. I live real fast here. In this business, quick is all that counts.

(**2 Troopers enter from behind The Big White Wall, pick up and sling on their weapons, & walk toward the river.**)

(**The Baby Rookie brandishes his weapon.**)
This, good people, is my own personal will. And my will says: who needs luck when you're quick as me. And you got one of these.

(**The Baby Rookie stomps onto the blue cloth. The 2 Tribe Men strain to lift it & release the river. The 2 Troopers grab the Tribe**

Men by their shoulders and topple them like freshly sawn trees.
The Tribe Men stiffen on their sides like tree limbs robbed of their
roots.)

I'm tellin' ya' I need no luck. I can zoom across any river you throw
my way with no luck at all.

(The Baby Rookie kicks away the cloth river. He blows a whistle
once. Each Trooper stabs a Tribe Man. Each Tribe Man exhales a
strong gust & then goes dark.)

There you go. Quick and fast. We burn through every river. No
luck involved in that at all.

(The Baby Rookie strides over to Mr. URUKUMU, grabs his flute,
breaks it & then looks down at him.)

First your voice goes, old man. Next I crack your sun in two.

(The Baby Rookie holds Mr. URUKUMU's head by his chin &
stares into his eyes.)

Was I there in your dream, old man? At night, behind your
eyeballs, did you see me?

(The 2 Troopers swagger over & flank Mr. URUKUMU. The Baby
Rookie gives a hand signal & the Troopers force down Mr.
URUKUMU's head. One of the Troopers also pins Mr.
URUKUMU with his foot.)

Could you smell me comin'? Did something dark fly across the
moon that night before ... us?

(The Baby Rookie signals & the Trooper removes his foot. The
Baby Rookie lifts Mr. URUKUMU's head by his hair & knocks off
the macaw headdress with a sweeping backhand.)

Just look at us ... we're nothing you could ever imagine. We walk through here bigger than your own gods.[2]

(The Baby Rookie drops Mr. URUKUMU's head.)
You're losing it all. It slips away from your hands, old man. We walk and breathe like kings while all of this just slips away from you. Forever. Gone now.

(Mr. URUKUMU rasps & chants:)

Mr. URUKUMU
Honi Xuma ... Honi Xuma ... Honi Xuma ... Honi Xuma ... Honi Xuma ...[3]

The Baby Rookie
(To Mr. URUKUMU:)
Too late for that. We got your Honi Xuma, too. Now, we're gonna' drink it all up.

(The Baby Rookie picks up the steaming bowl, smells it, cups a hand / pours out a palm-full & takes a drink. He makes a bitter face. Mr. URUKUMU watches – with a broad smile across his face – as The Baby Rookie drinks.)

Yeeech! How do you gag this swill down?
(Pause.) But drink it, we're a'gonna', and now we're drinking down your last secret, too. And we can see through your eyes, now. Everything you see, we see, now, too.

Mr. URUKUMU
So that's what you think? I just gotta' say: hang onto your ride, Cuz. Now, you're gonna' need it while you become what you see, what you feel, what you hear ...

223

The Baby Rookie
(Passes bowl to other Troopers & they take turns slurping down "the swill." Pokes URUKUMU hard with toe of his boot.)
The hell you say!

Mr. URUKUMU
Honi Xuma ... Honi Xuma ... Honi Xuma ... Honi Xuma ...

The Baby Rookie
(To Mr. URUKUMU who continues to chant.)
Indeed, old man, indeed. Say lookit' this: the Mother of Boas. We got your Boa Woman, too.

(The Baby Rookie pushes The Boa Woman toward the other Troopers. They toss away the bowl & begin to paw The Boa Woman.)
Maybe that's the last one, old man. Your last Boa Woman ... and we got her pinned. Even the skin of a Boa can't buy luck like we got.

(The Baby Rookie moves away from this debased action – though normally, he'd be right in the thick of it. But he's been there / done that, more or less. Maybe he'd like to think he & The Boa Woman shared something way more meaningful than this snatch & grab/push-fuck rigmarole he's trying not to watch. Maybe their experience left him too well shook-up for another go-round. Maybe he's just too tired to get it up again, so soon: & that's the official reason why he's not inclined to jump back into this recreational interlude with the other Troopers & "their" Boa. He lights a smoke, watches, laughs, and speaks to them in the spirit of "go along to get along.")
Save me some.

(2 Troopers take turns pawing The Boa Woman. They rip her skin, slap & fondle her. The Boa Woman kicks one of the Troopers – bulls-eye, two times right in his groin - & lands a

sweeping southpaw roundhouse square on the other's jaw. Both of them are smoked & left in the dirt. Then The Boa Woman launches herself at The Baby Rookie, leaps onto his back & cranks down on his neck in a choke-hold with her forearms. They struggle. One of the Troopers recovers, grabs his weapon, sights into The Boa Woman & shoots her twice at an angle to avoid penetrating The Baby Rookie's back. In a situation like this, hey: these guys need each other. Instrumentally, at least.)

(The Boa Woman slumps against The Baby Rookie's back. He gently lowers her to the ground. She folds back into herself & exhales a hard gust of breath.)

(The Baby Rookie picks up his weapon & points it at the Trooper who fired.)
The last one ... maybe so. Goddamn you! You just killed maybe the last Boa Woman.
I oughta' blow your balls straight off.
(Pause.) You don't need 'em now.

(The Baby Rookie lowers his weapon, kneels down at the side of The Boa Woman, touches her wounds, tastes her blood, smears some of it on his face.)
(To himself.) Go on. Stroke the Boa's skin, just for the luck of it.
(Laughs & speaks through his eerie joy-laughter:)
That's some kind of luck, no? That's all the luck you can ever hope to use.
(Pause.) The last one. Damn your balls.

(The other Trooper launches a strong kick to the back of the Trooper who killed The Boa Woman. The kicked Trooper goes down with the other Trooper on top of him. Both draw their combat knives. They struggle & cut each other deep.)

(Mr. URUKUMU changes the tempo of this action with slow rasping, with tongue clicks & his claves. The *Tree of Masks* erupts into tooth, claw, wind & wing sounds. And the sound of water. Everything you'd expect in such a situation.)

(2 Troopers on the ground writhe, groan & bleed out. The Baby Rookie cups his palms over his ears – his face shows terror.)

(Mr. URUKUMU blows through the mic'ed / tonally distorted PVC (or didgeridoo). The Baby Rookie goes down in pain & thrashes around. The *Tree of Masks* bursts into action. The Tribe Men yowl, whoop, growl, flow across the space & eddy around the dying Troopers. The Tribe Men pull off their masks: underneath, their faces are divided into red & white sectors – Like Mr. URUKUMU's. The Boa Woman unfolds & rises up from the dead with an agenda. She looms over The Baby Rookie.)

(Mr. URUKUMU ends his tempo/tone experiments abruptly. He grabs The Baby Rookie by his hair & lifts up his head so he can stare directly into The Boa Woman's face. She comes closer to him, holds his cheeks in her palms, moves even closer, kisses him once, then neatly twists his neck until it breaks. She drops his head like a rotten potato. The Boa Woman glides back to her first GO position & folds back into herself.)

(Mr. URUKUMU straps on his Telecaster, holds his hands above his head, briefly, nods to the Tribe Men, uncorks a power chord arpeggio & begins a repetitive, industrial thrash riff, surging with harmonic reverb. The Tribe Men hoist up the dying Troopers & seemingly dead Baby Rookie & toss them together in an old-school mosh pit. The Tribe Men beat out rhythm with their hands – on legs, on cheeks, on the ground as the Troopers & The Baby Rookie *mosh* like zombies: mechanically / spasmodically & violently against each other as Mr. URUKUMU plays. He stops abruptly & they collapse – like trees sawed-off from their roots – to the floor of the forest.)

Though these friendly fire melees are hardly what he must have envisioned when he made this statement, General George S. ("Our Blood, His Guts") Patton once said: "Battle is the most magnificent competition in which human beings can indulge." Indulge? Indeed!

But this is not much of a battle, is it? And this is hardly a war, either. It's more like bald-faced extortion as an arm of economic expansion, an outreach policy of "pacification," assimilation / absorption, or, if all that fails to gel, simple elimination. Aka ethnic cleansing / genocide / snuffing out and totally appropriating this unworthy Other's stash of land and resources, good marketable stuff and collective cultural memories. And this action is – on its surface – asymmetrical, though not in the way we normally construe that term applied to violence and mayhem.

The Terror waged by a weaker enemy against the civilian population of their more powerful oppressor can inspire fear and transmit paranoia. That's what we're used to seeing, now, in the world as we have made it. This "normal" Terror can paralyze the stronger power's social routines, and weaken morale and political resolve, but that's always a gamble. It could also galvanize a massive retaliation with collective punishment of anyone socially / politically / culturally tied in any way (however tangential) to the terrorists. And it also inspires intense genocidal hatred. Repeated acts of terror can make a bad situation, even more intractable.

But that dynamic also works much the same coming from the other - equally asymmetrical - direction: Massive Power thrown against a relatively weak enemy. So what else could you call something like Shock & Awe but Terror as a tactical policy? Or Terror as an emblematic image implanted into the dreams (waking or sleeping) of a weaker so-called foe, ripe for the plucking.[4]

Would it be meet and just to call The Baby Rookie a terrorist? What's he's doing certainly fits the pattern. It's no massive revelation, here, but what does The Baby Rookie really know? He seems to be wearing some sort of uniform, but does he really understand who or what he works for? I doubt he has the clearance to get that kind of "intel." He may not have the background to process what little he is given. We've seen something of his origins and training (in symbolic terms, anyway); we can sense his commitment to some loosely framed mission and that usually implies, at least, some belief in what you're doing - by agency and choice: and really, what's the practical difference.

Can The Baby Rookie make his way through this moral maze alone? Critical thought is never part of the Big Bad Who's agenda for the rest of us. And he's no different. But still we try, and maybe The Rookie needs to try harder. We must draw our own conclusions. I'm more inclined to side with Tarrou's.

(Mr. URUKUMU approaches The Baby Rookie. He turns him over, holds his head up by the chin & speaks into his vacant face:)

Mr. URUKUMU
So where are you off to now, Rookie?
It looks like your dream is done for,
It looks like your will and your luck
Your big-bad mojos, smack-talk and all,
Just flat ran out of juice
And all you got left now's a big fat lack.
Are you cut loose: do you swim or sleep or crawl,
- How do you cope, now? -
Through all the long far drift of history:
Are you gonna' be the star of the next act
Of history's next waking dream,
The kin of sun and stars and moon, or not?
Or will you just lay down here and rot
With the rest of us / with the best of we-all
Back into the burnt forest
Back into the dead sea
Back into the broken city
Back into the dookie bin
With all the other mopes
And clever – but degraded - widgets

From way-on-back before the fall
Back with all your played out dreams and sad debris?
So I'm just sayin': all ya'all can only hope 'cuz
Lack of hope is still the only sin that counts,
The only way to really stall the engine,
The only way to really fail,
When more's the pity,
When they gnash and rail against it all,
When they burn the mountain down,
With history's steady pulse set: on redial - on redial - on redial,
When all the counting's done
(Lights down.)

7
Undertaker, Undertaker Cut My Hair

(Welcome to The Baby Rookie's strange little wake. The scene we're watching is as still and silent as it was before it began. A mental "dialogue" of sorts soon happens between The Baby Rookie & The Boa Woman, primarily to trigger changes in The Rookie's internal landscape – personal priorities, moods & preferences, metaphysics / superstitions, political biases & assumptions that mold one's perception of justice or freedom / all the self-referential terms of art for free-floating fragments of vestigial, frayed & worn-out, largely forgotten (but still able to activate) personality engrams that we've heard mentioned before & talked about ourselves, as well, so often. This silent process happens before his coming ascension or crashing/go-smash descent. The best thing we can do, I guess, is silently to bear witness to their shared, motionless silence. Something significant is going on beneath the detection levels of our sensory array. We need to trust the process & see what comes next. It takes the form of this little tune The Boa Woman sing-whispers into The Baby Rookie's ear. Figuratively, of course.)

Undertaker Song

Undertaker
Undertaker
Cut my hair
Long time / long time
Bum and ice
Down here
Kick it over hard
Still as nothing stands
Here where God does-not-care
Undertaker
Undertaker
Cut my hair

Undertaker
Undertaker
Cut my hair
Long time
Ol' zoo-lion in a cage
Down here
Too much jagged
Heavy turn around
Pulse between we cannot bear
Undertaker
Undertaker
Cut my hair

Undertaker
Undertaker
Cut my hair
Long time
Wrecked my own head
In this storm down here
Lookin' back, I don't

Runnin' blind, I am
Burn down every thing, I dare
Undertaker
Undertaker
Cut my hair

(On the surface, this mise-en-scène looks exactly the same as it did at the start. The Baby Rookie still lays in a bloody heap slightly downstage center from The Big White Wall. The Boa Woman remains where & as we left her, previously: adamant, arcane, stolid, covert, impenetrable, etc. – hunched over & folded into herself, but still bloody or, perhaps, still bleeding. Like most of life, this surface gestalt – shiny/happy, or just ordinarily bleak/uninspiring, or even flat-opaque/extraordinarily unrevealing - is all we can expect. But in this case, we've got better intel.)

8
"Wake Up Dead Man"

(Not to beat up a dead horse, too much, but "The Baby Rookie still lays in the same bloody heap a bit downstage center from The Big White Wall." The Boa Woman remains where & as we left her, previously: adamant, arcane, stolid, covert/impenetrable, etc. Hunched over & folded into herself. Still bloody or, perhaps, still bleeding. Someome has finally dragged the bodies of the other Troopers away from view. Who knows who / who knows why? Otherwise, there's nothing new here this time, either.)

(His Fucking Dummy sits downstage-left in a director's chair made from some sort of exotic hardwood; perhaps this wood was harvested from his own locale. We hope not, but one thing is probably certain: if the finished wood was made from logs harvested in this forest, His Fucking Dummy's people most

231

certainly got no benefit from the chain of business transactions that made that happen.)

(His Fucking Dummy wears a T-shirt that shows his true colors: *Yo Soy un Defensor de la Selva*. He's reading a copy of The Guardian (in Portuguese) & is tracking the efforts of the WHO and NGO's like the Rainforest Action Network / Greenpeace / Survival International and others to ensure (as much as they could ever do so) that *isolados* among indigenous peoples in this region are safely sequestered from outsiders – of any political / religious stripe – while the corona virus is burning a swath through the Americas. And after, even, unless they want to help develop a health / energy / educational infrastructure for tribes that want these things. With NO strings attached! His Fucking Dummy doesn't seem too very much fascinated by the fate of The Baby Rookie – hardly giving the scene of carnage even a fleeting side-eye glance. He's got other / bigger fish to fry.)

(Mr. URUKUMU walks into the scene from one side or the other. He scopes the gestalt, inspects certain aspects of the details, and moves slowly from one side to the other. He touches The Boa Woman's forehead, sort of like a gentle call to wake-up & arise. The Boa Woman full-body shivers. Her limbs move like shaking off a poisonous sleep, or a a dose of some barbituate laced with sodium pentathol. She stretches and watches Mr. URUKUMU's progress, tracking the progress of his inspection tour. Her eyes light on The Baby Rookie: she tenses up & freezes.)

(The Baby Rookie comes to with an obvious jolt. He's eyes bug out & open up. He tries to rise but his body fails him. He's overtaken by a fit of nervous overflow. His dawning consciousness looks to us like a steadily escalating wave of pain. He tries to talk / cry out / give forth an anguished scream, but his tongue appears to be locked, his scream is totally visual / but still striking in its own hideous way. He locks into this postion.)

(Urukumu motions for The Boa Woman to follow him & she does. They stand on either side of The Baby Rookie. Mr. URUKUMU smacks The Rookie's forehead three times & his tongue loosens up. He speaks through & around a series of full-body spasms, apparently unaware of the others:)

The Baby Rookie

I ... I ... I ... I'm still here? I ... dreamed ... I ... I ... I ... I was ... I was ...

Mr. URUKUMU

(Takes The Baby Rookie's chin in his hand & speaks directly into him:)
It was no dream. You just been somewhere even I've never seen. Listen close, listen to me. (Pause.) It-was-no-dream.

The Baby Rookie

(Progressively ever more agitated, he sees Mr. URUKUMU:)
You! You ... I ... I'm still here? Still here ... Me ... You! ... I'm still here. (The Baby Rookie Rookie shifts gears.) I... I'm still here. I ... I ... it was a joke. Just a joke. It was all ... a jo/ke

The Boa Woman

(Grabs The Baby Rookie's head out of Mr. URUKUMU's grasp & stares into his face. She, too, speaks into him, but it's more like spitting:)
No joke, motherfucker! You joke and people die! Many-many-myriads of. People. Die. People die-die-die: it's a big chain of yesterday-today-tomorrow. All that time people just die. Because of your sick joke? You think that's funny? Ha-fucking-ha-ha-ha!

Mr. URUKUMU

(Snorts out a laugh of sorts:) So how far you gonna' go with this so-called joke?
You are mos def not now surfing down the Ave back in the old home-town / back on the "ol' main drag" on a banana peel. In fact, I know, a goon like you has got some things of great significance to

233

spit out, own and claim. In fact, you've got so many in-famous things of some real significance to reveal / admit / disclose, and soon, soon, you're gonna' go there.

(Mr. URUKUMU motions to The Boa Woman & together they hoist the stricken Baby Rookie up onto his wobbly legs. Together they force him to his knees & splay his arms like a St. Andrew's Cross – nothing religious or symbolic or symbolically religious here, they just like the shape and that very shape facilitates the next piece of action. The Boa Woman stands behind The Baby Rookie to keep his arms outstretched & maintain that shape. He looks kind of like a bug pinned to a bug display board (or a "patient etherized upon a table," so the old song goes). And The Baby Rookie is frozen / rigid, now. His eyes are still bugged open / his mouth hangs slack / his tongue, no longer locked, lolls about like a hound dog's.)

Mr. URUKUMU

So you think you been living your own story for a long time now. Well ... so have we. Maybe your story is your own world of possibility, or maybe it's not. But it sure as hell is not gonna' be ours. So I'm telling you, listen hard, the message comes to you from outside the mainframe, pre-packaged in your very own jagged barracks / jail-house / cartel courier crude-blunt bludgeon lingo. Just so's ya' knows. I can do this better / I can do this more uptown but, instead, I'm walking downtown with it, cuz' I really want to get through to you.

(Pause.) Someday, someday soon, you're gonna' see your own face plastered on some year's / maybe this year's Pulitizer Prize-winning atrocity poster, your big gun still smokin', big grin splayed out across your face for all to see, your big mug frozen in the frame, famous now – you want that kind of fame? - easy-peasy pickin's for any Big Bad Who, or Who's minions, to spin and throw flim-flam all around the crime you did for Him and them. See, when all the smoke blows away, and your cover dries up and "it's time to pay it down" comes down on your own head, then you got to find your secret face, your hidden other - li -ness, your first face, the one you forgot you ever remembered before you were dead. Cuz' then it's all up to you to take their fall on your own. They are gonna' just walk away, stalk away like bulbous-fatty-sweaty satraps, blabbing at the cameras: **(And here Mr.URUKUMU does his best impersonation of The Rookie's best, but merely approximate, conception of The Big Bad Who, Himself:)** "Hey, I don't know shit, I don't know who or what or when about no crime. Hey, if I told you once, I told you two times, and I ain't sayin' it again - and it ain't no fuckin' question: who the fuck is this person? I don't know nothing about this person. This so-called-actual-person? Really! And this person – this fucking-so-called person! - ain't no friend of mine at all."[6]

(Pause.) And you might think you're so immune, well, no-no Baby Rookie, you're just so naive, you're a bad cartoon made to crash while the Big Who's do their uber-do's, make hash of our dreams and hang out in their insulated bubbles, way up above, far from your pain ... and mine. So ... don't send me none of your love, or your troubles. So don't come to my house looking for yourself because you ain't there either. I am / not you! This time, it's high time to come clean, talk, feel what you mean, parlay with your own dichotomy. You don't need to pretend ... to really listen to this next part ... to understand a goddamn thing, this time. Now, you're just a'gonna' feel it all, hard and loud and long.

(While The Boa Woman maintains her grasp on The Baby Rookie's outstetched slightly upward arms, Mr. URUKUMU adjusts his head / neck / shoulders to maximize the graspability, clarity, directness & transparency of an immanent stream of upcoming / incoming transmissions – which he will inadvertently channel. Finally, he pulls The Baby Rookie's tongue out for a final "tongue check" – see, he did learn something from that last colonial pretty-talk training session in the woods. *Zoophile*! That was his clear favorite, followed closely by *shillelagh*! Mr.

235

URUKUMU scrapes the crust of his coma off The Baby Rookie's tongue & tunes it up for the task at hand. Then he steps back & The Rookie is ready to roll:)

(As this stream of glossolalic / multi-national speech unreels from The Baby Rookie's mouth, The Big White Wall becomes a screen for a another stream: visual images that occasionally reinforce or clarify / but just as often refute or belie what's rolling off his mouth. Some persist longer than others / some are done & gone relatively quickly. A less than exhaustive list of these images might include: 1) Outside shot of Federal Immigration Detention Center (Hudson NJ). 2) Nickel ore smelter stack spewing smoke and particulates (on shore of Lake Izabel, Guatemala), 3) Law enforcement hosing down Dakota pipeline blockade activists with water during period of near-freezing temperatures with Standing Rock Sioux (at Cannon Ball, North Dakota). 4) Flower vendors (all women) clash with troops and federal police when they were blocked from selling flowers in the Texcoco market (San Salvador Atenco, Mexico). 5) A large red stain across the surface of Lake Izabel. 6) A wide angle shot of the Federal Detention Center (at Tornillo, Texas) / cut to another wide angle shot of the Federal Detention Center (at Dilley Texas). 7) A wall of flames engulfing a section of rain forest (in Mato Grosso State, Brazil). 8) Mexican troops attempting to contain a wall of Zapatista women (at Chenalho, Chiapas, Mexico). 9) A subway car in New York City powered, staffed and maintained by essential transit workers / carrying a load of essential workers in other industries during the corona virus lockdown (New York City, NY / USA). 10) Heavy brownish dust in the air above a surface mining operation that engulfs / obscures an indigenous village (in Oaxaca, Mexico) / cut to heavy red dust that envelops & obscures the main steet/highways out of an indigenous village (El Pairaso, Guatemala). 11) A wide angle group portrait of indigenous children in the Brazilian Amazon. 12) A full face portrait of Brazilian ethno-journalist, **Sebastião Salgado**, with a banner underneath: "... we are facilitating the entry of coronavirus ... this

236

is genocide ... it would mean the extinction of Brazil's indigenous people." 13) A wide angle shot of scene from film – "At Play in the Fields of the Lord" – showing the agony of an indigenous village inadvertently infected with a respiratory virus by evangelical missionaries / cut to a closer view near the center of the village, multi-family structures & large groups of immobile bodies are visible / cut to an even closer view that features the carnage in a single, multi-family structure – faces, distorted by air hunger & fear, bodies in disarray. 14) An ICU filled to overflowing with COVID-19 patients (New York City, NY / USA). 15) A mass grave for COVID-19 victims (outside Tehran, Iran). 16) Migrant workers seeking to return home are herded into groups, made to stand while sanitation crews spray them with a strong bleach solution as a COVID precaution (at a state–to-state border in rural India). 15) The signature / eponymous / & infamous shot of Iraqi prisoner in stress position, maintaining rigidity to avoid electrocution (in Abu Ghraib prison, Bagdad / Iraq). 17) Photo of grave diggers / cemetery attendants in Haz-Mat suits with coffins (in Manaus, State of Amazonia / Brazil) / jump cut to aerial shot of trenches used as mass graves with stacked body bags & coffins (in Manaus, State of Amazonia / Brazil). 18) Still from demo-video of proper water-boarding technique used on actual prisoner (at Guantanamo Prison, Cuba – but never officially claimed by the USA / note: video compiled for training & quality control / quality assurance purposes). 19) A single boot, half-buried in sand – found in debris after carnage from artillery barrage and carpet bombing (in an unnamed village in Northern Syria / outside Mosul in Iraq / in the Bekaa Valley in Lebanon / in the ... This image was more or less recommended by *El Sup*, himself.)

The Baby Rookie Talk-Stream / Crypto-Monologue (Part 1)

(This stream of urgency is strictly a frame of suggestions. Of course there's some chance in the process & not all of these channels will light up circuits in The Baby Rookie's brain - & make their way into his mouth:)

It's January the 1st / *Papi, ¿por que lloras?* / Who is ... who is ... who is the moral hazard here / the mountain is eating our village / hey, now it's your turn on the slab / 5 bucks an hour – 2 hours a grave: dig, slag, dig / the sky opened up: like the wound of a knife / helicopters and airplanes flew across the sky / the Amazon is not burning, not burning at all / you might at least pretend to listen / the mine is eating the mountain, too / *tocar o fogo* / take up the bodies – stack 'em three high *en la trinchera*, like wood / *con nuestras manos crudas* / they were afraid us dead would walk again / all day, every day and into the night: fear smells strong: a loud machine / we are dead and at war again / we are on a hunger strike: Give us toilet paper and soap / I'm a'gonna' uncork the kraken on your ass / right here, there is the virus / so who get's to hole up and isolate? / dig-slag-dig! / who get's fed to the virus talkin' / *Papi, ¿por que lloras?* / vultures are part of the ecosystem, too, no? / these deaths are not random – these deaths are targets / they come in screaming, they beat us like cows: Why? Why? We don't break any laws / *¡morder ese dolor!* / these deaths are targeted deaths / It's January the 1st, again / we will last, here, until we don't / what's their word for us: that word, how does that word work its dark magic? / dig-slag-dig-slag-dig-slag-dig! / lot's of us are sick, here / gasoline, oil, metal, gunpowder: loud machines that all smell like fear / a red stain spread across the lake like a bad rash / guards get hand sanitizer – we get 1 bar of soap a week for each cell – if we can buy it / *este é um genocídio necessário* / I hit him – a bunch of times, over and over – I put his head in a phone book and hit him over and over / *se é um índio tomá-lo* / whole areas – once green, once humid – now they're dry and bare / many people have died on the road from this mine / tie her up to the "parrot's perch": go-bouncy-bouncy-bouncy / *si es india, tiralo* / the bruises don't show up if you use an old phone book, a big one / here's a litany of batshit-crazy backwards: thieves run free – truth hunted down / hey, now it's your turn on the slab / I could never do such things to people / criminals judge me – the most gets more and more and more / I cry at dog-food commercials / *si es indio, tiralo* / I'm not wired to hurt you / our real work ... our real work is preparing to capture the next town / don't make me

238

hurt you / the ore trucks run them over – the trucks don't stop / I'm a'gonna crush yer' balls, boy / the least has nothing-loses more and more and more / *se é um índio matá-lo* / sky opens up: like the wound of a knife / you should all disappear / to make us disappear – you must disappear / people look alive but don't feel – don't move – can't think – can't talk – can't do anything: are they really dead / it is always, now, forever / it's January the 1st / you're making me hurt you, again / *¡de vuelta en la tormenta vas!* ... *Papi, ¿por que lloras?*

(The Baby Rookie shakes in spasms. He makes noise from his mouth as if trying to speak. Eventually, this noise clarifies into something we can all understand.)

The Baby Rookie

What ... what the fuck ... (Pause) ... Oh! Oow! Goddamn I really hurt ... my head's fucking coming unglued. Even my fucking thoughts hurt ... each new one hurts more than the last one ... Oh God! ... are these really MY thoughts?

(The Baby Rookie groans & sags a bit, still in The Boa Woman's firm grasp. If his arms & hands were free & he had some range of motion, he'd certaintly be holding his head in his palms & rocking back & forth, still moaning, of course.)

Mr. URUKUMU

Got me, but the rest makes sense. Thoughts are, at the very least, a physical phenomenon. And sometimes, they ought to really hurt. At the very most, it's quite a bit more complicated. Like measuring the atomic weight of a single soul. Or the surface tension in a mother's tear, the tensile warp across an orphan's belly, stretched by years of hunger – food can never even touch that kind of hunger. Or the half-life of an ancient, nagging fear. (Straight through that Fourth Wall again.) See: finally, my time as a Behaviorist comes in handy, already.

The Baby Rookie

Wha ... what are you babbling about? Stop talking shit. What's happening to me. Why won't this yak-yak-stream stop? Did I go to Hell, or what?

(Pause. The Baby Rookie shakes, seems to be wracked by spasms of pain? Of empathy? Or revulsion (self / other)? Or a personal ontological tectonic upheaval? Or all of that, simultaneously?)

Am I there, now? Right now? Where do these voices come from?

Mr. URUKUMU

Where they go when you can't hear them is more the question, no?
(Pause.)
No? I guess that's not a hair you're fixin' to split. Well look at that, would you!

(Mr, URUKUMU points over toward His Fucking Dummy's official observation post. The Guardian is gone, his computer is folded up and sleeping for the rest of the evening. He displays a sign, first for our benefit, and then he tilts it at a better angle into The Baby Rookie's view. The sign says: *"I'm Sending You Back To The Thinking Room.*[7] Mr. URUKUMU grabs The Baby Rookie's head & steers his vision toward the Dummy's sign. This mention of the *"thinking room"* refers to a very crude, old-school colonial methodology for recovering (or covering over, rather) / restructuring memory / and implanting new goals & desires more in lock-step with the needs of an empire. But that's not to be The Baby Rookie's fate, here. The Rookie fixates on that sign, attempting to crane his neck for a better line of sight, but it's obvious from his tortured expression that he hasn't the foggiest, most rudimentary notion what it means, or where he's supposed to go with it.)**

What a fine suggestion. I think he's spot on, and so's: back inside this story – maybe possible / maybe not – you go's. This story's got some real legs. It's got it's feet on the ground and maybe, just maybe, part of this story is your story, too. See if you can catch up with this story, before it outruns your life. This time listen like a bare wire: throbbing, aching, open to the mercy or cruelty of the world. This time let the story empty you out: 'til the fight inside stops. Don't come back until you figure out where all these shadows come from. Shadows in-between ... you know ... the blank spots where people used to be. Then you tell me, I'd like to hear your uncut feelings. What you haven't stepped on yet.

(Mr. URUKUMU jerks The Baby Rookie's head back to his original, oracular (for want of a better word) position – sort of like throwing him back into the deep end of the pool while he's wearing a pair of pretty heavy cement booties. Mr. URUKUMU gives him a few last exhortatory phrases to chew on:)

And I really hope you weren't expecting a Tin Man's testimonial tick-tock. No-No-No, you harsh-crude marauder / you bold destroyer of worlds: it's time to jump back inside that stochastic matrix of currents and counter-currents, talkin' and doin' / talkin' and doin' and embrace your death, yet again. Someone / somewhere should get some use out it all, no? Go Then:

(Again, The Big White Wall serves as a screen for – this time – a very few specific images. 1) Zapatista women leaning on their heavy sticks, waiting to defend their village should the army come to launch an assault. 2) A young Zapatista girl looks into the camera for a portrait – she's wearing a brightly embroidered mask and at the top of of the mask – between her mouth and her nose is the word, *Ella*. 3) A phalanx of strong left arms – Zapatista women in a long line of arms & profiles. 4) A Zapatista woman with a sock puppet – maybe like a Teatro Campesino in Chiapas – during campaign to pass International Referendum for the Recognition of Indigenous Rights & Culture / an end to the War of Extermination. 5) *El Sup's* famous image of the boot (back again like an irritating bad penny), abandoned in the sand after a battle: mate-less, forsaken, no foot to wear it ergo no where to go. This last image remains on the screen for the duration of The Baby

Rookie's time here, all alone, with the physical manifestation of the boot. Did I say that's coming too, and very quickly?)

Does the fact that no one in any of these images looks remotely like The Baby Rookie bother him? Should it? Well, we think it should, and quite a bit. Even though he's facing away from the screen, these images are ingredients in the flow of talk-talk / invective / simple declaration / exhortation / denunciation and lament moving right through him and into the aethers of the political space. None of the people we see through him share his specific circumstances, either – except perhaps the soldiers – on either side – in the battle for Falujah that may have played (on that same screen) in his nursery, back-a-days. Or the War in the Falkland Islands / Malvinas reprise that played – just for him, he may have thought – in his own living room when he was just about in junior high.

But those were actual wars – few would argue with that call. "Official" wars with all their grisly bona fides. And these other images seem to come from conflicts beyond that circumstantial pale. On second thought, maybe, they're not so different, regardless of how they look on their surfaces.

We've had something like this conversation before - about power imbalances / assymetical tactics / terror and the like. I haven't made up my own mind yet, but I'm still thinking. How about you? And don't you wonder how The Rookie feels about what he's seeing / saying. What he, himself, has just been deeply involved in all this time? Like where does he really stand? It all comes down to nothing but questions, & more questions. But while questions may enhance the nuances and tip-toe gingerly across Occam's reliably sharp razor, ultimately, actions do trump questions. Just as actions transmute fears. So where is this going? Like ... where?

(And a brand new talk-stream now pours forth from The Baby Rookie's mouth. The rhetoric and organization of this next stream is more pointed, perhaps, more distinct. No longer served up at the speed & pitch of a scream. There are fewer disjunctions, less

despair, but the content is equally urgent. He says it as it comes to & through him. As before, not every option here will make the cut:)

The Baby Rookie's Talk-Stream / Crypto-Monologue (Part 2)

It's January the 1st / Many people have died here but this is our home / who ... just who is the moral hazard here / you ... you made us possible / you made us necessary / you made us grow

Our work here is knocking down the 4th wall of the political space / to show – how it really is / on the inside – where all that theatre goes on / inside, there on the side / where you said we don't belong / so who ... who is the moral hazard, here

Tocar o fogo / behind us are all of you / all of us-you-we / our mask is a mirror / who do you see in the mirror

Behind our masks is you / *detrás de nuestra mascaras eres tu*

It's January the 1st, again / our work here is finding all the cracks, all the tiny little networks of cracks / all the cracks in all the pretty pictures/ cracks in the grand scheme of what it is / but only on the outside / our work here is prying open all the cracks in the pretty outsides

Behind our masks are you / *detrás de mascaras son ustedes*

Helipcopters and airplanes flew across the sky / fear – you could smell it there / fear that all us dead would walk again / the air below smells good, smells fresh / the air above smells like fear / the air below smells like hope / and we are from below / us and many like us from below / fear above – the dead below / and on this day, the dead smell like hope / *¡Nuestras fuerzas, nuestra palabra!*

243

¡Ya Basta!: to conformity / to cynicism / to apathy / to the gods of ego, war and theirves / to the laws of acquisition, absoption and decay

We are your Other / your dead ringer, but backwards / what's behind the smoke you made to hide what you do / you, that smoke you made makes us grow stronger / to make us disappear – you must disappear

a cobra não cuida do índio / it's January the 1st, again, yet again / and we dead / of all times, dying, once again / to live / to live more

Tocar o fogo / It's January the 1st / *genocídio contra os isolados é inaceitável*/ we take care of our land

esse genocídio é inaceitável / *¡Ya basta!* / who is the moral hazard here?

¡Nuestras fuerzas, nuestra palabra!' / At dawn we had taken the city / by noon, we prepared to take the next

We live / we all live in an ocean of little worlds / our work here is building / building / a whole new good world / building a world many little worlds fit into

You made us / you made us grow / you gave us deep roots / to make us disappear, you must disappear / we must all disappear

A boot in the sand, a boot without a mate / without a foot to put inside it / without a place to go / without a reason to be there, in the sand / empty / another last thing left after bombs rain down / an empty boot / waiting to be filled up / *tocar el fuego*

It's always, now and forver, January the 1st / *tocar el fuego*

(The talk-stream stops, but the image of the boot remains. The Baby Rookie star stares ahead, slack-jawed, again, until Mr.

URUKUMU cuffs him – once / twice / again - & he more or less resucitates enough to mouth a question, or rather more than one:)

The Baby Rookie
Where am ... I am still here? (The Rookie sees himself, perhaps for the first time from this POV.) But ... but my hands ... look at what's all over my hands ... I don't know how / I got ....

Mr. URUKUMU
(At /.) What you hear, what you say, even what you do from now on, doesn't get your hands clean. They're gonna' stay that way for a long time ... maybe, forever.

The Baby Rookie
These words ... I hear them in my head before they leap out of my mouth. These words are not my words. Are they? Where ... who did this intel come from?

Mr. URUKUMU
Don't be so sure of that. Who can own a word? What a dumb bunny's idea. No one owns these words then they must belong to everyone, or no one at all.
(Pause.)
Stop calling everything you don't understand, intel. This was not intel, gathered on the sly. Not a briefing, or a satellite transmission from some sky-net. Hah and Hell-No! These words are direct dispatches from our shared old world past, into our badly-shafted / fully-grifted new world present – boiling over, half craft and guile / half straight from our guts, and, full of bloody jagged edges – with at least one toe in our collective receding future ... our new world, our next world. O-Yeah! / O-Yeah!! And what a jewel to fight and die for, don'tcha' think?

(Mr. URUKUMU places both of his hands on The Baby Rookie's sagging shoulders & looks him in the eyes.)

The Baby Rookie

Fight who? For what? I'm tired. I hurt. I am really ... just tired. I could sleep for twenty years.

Mr. URUKUMU

Someday, maybe, but no sleep now for you. You listened this time – at least I hope you did – so now you should know where your score stands. Stale, pale, or garish, even transfigurational, these shards of talk-talk-talk, these images – floating by like fiery balloons - these clips of actions – choked desires, some aborted / some fully strapped, some locked-down, withering on the tree, left to their own bleak destinies, decorate the walls of the cave inside your head like a codex, like some glossary from an ancient tongue. Or a user's manual mashed together with quack diagnoses, old-school horoscopes, a coroner's hasty inquest – before anyone looks too hard – a ledger of the last decade's total flow of clean and dirty business, a tract, maybe some kinda' scripture. All stuff you can use. You get that, no?

The Baby Rookie

Get that? Get ... use ... what? All I know is I'm tired. My head is fried. My bones are too heavy, my whole body's too loose, now, to lift me up. **(Pause. The Rookie sees himself, again.)** Look ... look at what's all over my hands! **(Pause.)** You know ... you know what I saw? I think I saw my own soul gone dark ... no shape ... my soul is homeless. It walked away from my body ... it looked back at me and all I could see was disgust ... I heard it say in disgust: fuck that body over there! That's not my body ... not no more! Then... I don't know how to say... then ... then my soul puked. My soul looked back at me / at my body and puked. I could hear it. **(Pause)** Look ... look at what's all over my hands! Goddamn me!

Mr. URUKUMU

That's always a possibility. But I think you're ready as you're ever gonna' be.

(Mr. URUKUMU gob-smacks himself (but lightly, almost just theatrically) & turns away from The Rookie. He's obviously frustrated, probably wondering why he first embarked on this seemingly-senseless, Quixotic project with me. I'm sure we'll have something tense to talk about when this last scene concludes.)

(The Boa Woman intervenes. She clamps a single palm over The Baby Rookie's mouth – while maintaining her point of leverage behind him with her other arm. This allows his limp arms to dangle freely – like a rag doll's. And then she speaks to him. This time, with not so much venom, not so much like spitting, but still severely: no soft edges, without compromise, no quarter given. Like she's schooling a recalcitrant mule but still has some faith in the mule's ability to learn and then do:)

The Boa Woman

This is, maybe, the last brick wall of unknowing
Still standing, and you've got to bore on through it.
Maybe this is the taste / feel / sound of your own soul being hacked.
Maybe this is not what you volunteered for, at all.
Maybe you just woke up in a big fear
from your long drawn-out haze
And discovered: hey, here I am
carrying a fucking spear in the Pharoah's army!
Maybe this is all coming into you, from the outside.
Imposed on you, projected through / into you, or
Maybe you forgot to check your blind spots
And just backed on into it: O what simple luck for you,
But maybe it's been in there, almost
Brimming, all along, inside you.
Maybe you'll come out of this really glad, again,
Just to be unhappy in your own uncolonized head.

Just to be unseen, again, with no name
No past, nothing today, not too much tomorrow
Up ahead for you, for simple you.
No where left for you to be led.
For unheard / unacknowledged / unloved / undesired you,
For plain and ordinary, unembellished you:
Maybe nothing much to look for today.
No cure / no way, but your own simple sorrow,
Your own sweet simple singularity:
No more simulation, nothing borrowed,
something actual for a change.
Maybe that's too simple, and it probably is for sure,
But the sun's gone behind, now,
And maybe, now, at least you know it's yours ...

(The Boa Woman stares soft daggers into The Rookie's eyes &
holds his head firmly like a gentle vice. She kisses him full on the
lips, breaks into & enters his mouth with her tongue & holds onto
him that way for a long moment. Then she speaks to him, again - a
cautionary note or two:)

Hey, don't get hot so quick on me, Baby Rookie.
Don't get no way no big ideas that make you so wet, so easy.
Spur of the spur of the moment: Hey,
I just made this up, on that you can bet.
Cuz, "every day is any day now," and you ain't seen nothin' yet.

(And now – mirabile dictu! - A single boot, imbedded in the sand
suddenly materializes before The Rookie's undeserving /
disbelieving eyes. There's wind, now, he's simultaneously in the
forest and the desert, at the bottom of a deep-old ocean watching
as the wind (or current) unearths a little more of the contours of
that single boot. And this boot holds his attention like nothing
else ever has. Like something formerly scorned but now fairly
blazing, miraculous, glorious, truly lasting, rising up from a pool of
sewage, a fence-line zone of no-go – full of cancer – next to a

248

refinery, a burned-down jungle, or the bombed wreckage of civilian neighborhoods in a once vibrant city / a formerly peaceful country town that both became military targets of opportunity. And simultaneously, like a curse he'll never even try to shake?)

So where did this boot of great portent actually come from? Did His Fucking Dummy toss his own boot into the ring when none of us were looking? Is this a ruse or a clue he's given us? Is it some other boot he stumbled on trekking through the forest to organize resistance to more theft, to future incursions? He must despise groups like whoever The Baby Rookie works for, and at this juncture, he probably knows more about their identities and agendas than The Rookie ever will.

Because the Rookie's privilege – it ain't much but it's still a whole lot more than The Dummy's (if in, fact His Fucking Dummy has any at all) - is like a veil or an imbedded / precisely engineered deep-cover identity. It clouds the places where he shouldn't look too deeply and saps his curiosity about the big questions. It cloaks the ground of his being in a big deep fog. And it also works like a sweet drug: dulling all the sharp edges of his very own, very tiny "real world" where he still sees himself as master, as sleek, smooth operator, as an indomitable world wrecker, or, again, as an innocent font of unlimited kindness and giving. And with any drug like that, lack of truly penetrating self-awareness is one of its steepest costs.

*So maybe we don't expect too much insight on The Rookie's part despite Mr. URUKUMU's best efforts at practical magic. But maybe we should expect / or, more to the point, maybe we should demand some real change. Who knows? Maybe Mr. URUKUMU actually had nothing to do with this apparition and he's just as blown away as The Baby Rookie seems to be. Maybe we've all just witnessed a truly extra-ordinary / paranormal event! I know this resort to **ex machina** explanations infuriates the raw-boned realists among us, but at least there will be no mention of any **deus** in the works.*

(Inspired by what's just "materialized," Mr URUKUMU turns back toward The Baby Rookie. Perhaps he feels a glimmer of hope,

now, that his efforts thus far are going to pay off in the long run. Perhaps, he's just amazed that such a thing could happen, right here / right now at perhaps the ripest teachable moment. Just a thought. I don't know what he's really thinking.)

Mr. URUKUMU

Wow! Behold, that there boot of destiny. That's a good one, no? The boot with no past, no mate, cast off / cast out from the blessed realm of all other boots. No foot to wear it ergo no where to go. For that boot, all the songs of glory are already sung. For that lonely boot, the war is most truly done and gone. No friends to trust but sand / sun / wind and these "friends" will wear that boot down to elemental dust. **(Pause.)**

So now that you've been there and back, Baby Rookie, wherever it is you've gone, who's words are you gonna' trust, and what are you gonna' do with that boot? Pull it up out of the sand? Pop it on and hop away looking for the other one? Tell us true: speaking with your brain, through your heart, in your own best words, right here in this place, this someone else's actual home, where you can't stay, where you'll never find yourself, but you will heal – because there's nothing left to do with all of this, but heal.

Mr. URUKUMU

(Takes his last parting shot at The Rookie:) So what do you say-do-think-feel, next? For you? For the boot? For *nosotros*? For the rest of it all? At least tell yourself that much: what comes next? And are you empty, too, are you empty, yet – inside to outside / downside to up – are you empty … under the sky?

(That's probably all that we'll see happen here. **Mr. URUKUMU** leaves for parts unknown – but I know I'll see him later, he's got a few bones to pick with me, and pick them clean, he will. That's just the way he's wired. The Boa Woman also evaporates – almost as quickly as the boot appeared. She's probably glad this gig is done. It's a lot to expect: all these unleavened waves of

250

overdramatized, toxic masculinity to swim against with no guarantee of change or movement to make it worth the wear & tear on her neurology. I'm fairly sure she needs to decompress & has many better places to be. And if anything of deep significance was revealed, well. maybe we blinked and this show is live so there's no rewind function to fall back on. So, maybe, we just missed it. But maybe the real show – the deep part - is just begining, now.)

(It's down to The Baby Rookie, all alone, with that single, scuffed-up, ill-used and abandoned boot, now. He's staring at it, and as we watch – are you still watching? – the boot seems to grow in size / stature / presence / emblematic & actual gravity. It almost positively looms directly in our line of sight, now. It's colonizing our vision / our image-making brains. He can't possibly miss what's going on square in his face while that short distance between The Rookie & the boot becomes a *terra incognita* No Man's Land for all the rest of us. So: will he rise to this challenge the boot throws down on him – it's just like passing him a strong slap. But could it also be a tentative kiss? That's the question: What's He Gonna' Do?)

More Later

Notes on the story of

The Baby's Rookie Year:

[1] From Franz Fanon's *"Wretched of the Earth."*

[2] Sometimes, but very occasionally, a stone-courageous / unusually idealistic soldier (and clearly, always, a rule deontologist) interrupts the silence and cracks open this *great-chain-of-violence-against-being* for clear public scrutiny. Like (then) Warrant Officer Hugh Thompson when he landed his Hiller-Raven gunship at Sơn Mỹ during the My Lai Massacre during the Vietnam War. He trained his guns on American soldiers from 1st Platoon / C Company (1st Battalion / 20th Infantry Regiment) under Lt. William Calley. He threatened to shoot them if they didn't stop executing civilians, immediately. By doing this, he stopped some of the killing – though, literally, many hundreds had been / were still gunned down and dumped into mass pits. He later gave an official account that found its way into Seymour Hersh's reportage on what came to be known as the *My Lai Massacre*.

Thompson's act upended his life – if you're going to blow the whistle, you've got to drink the hemlock. He was ostracized by the military and demonized by much of civilian society. Simultaneously, Calley was lionized as a patriotic meme - before such things existed as memes. Thompson experienced a host of problems often associated with readjustment after such an ambiguous / ethically fraught / asymmetrical conflict: PTSD (which didn't yet exist as a diagnostic category for him), alcoholism, dysfunction in his marriage, and nightmare disorder.

Thirty years after the fact, Thompson and his crew were awarded the Soldiers Medal for bravery. His name, however, remains a footnote (just like this one). And his act of heroism, and its consequences, a cautionary tale from a number of different perspectives.

Hugh Thompson and, I suppose, the rest of his crew are dead now. Seymour Hersh – after a long career of disemboweling official lies and reading their guts like an ancient augur – most recently brought to light the atrocities at Abu Ghraib Prison - has since gone relatively dark. And surprisingly few people even remember Lt. Calley. He was originally convicted in a military court and sentenced to life in prison for these war crimes. His sentence was soon reduced to 20 years (Military Court of Appeals), then to 10 years (Secretary of the Army). In response to popular patriotic outcry, he was later given a greatly reduced stretch of three years under house arrest (by Order of President Richard Nixon / 1974).

But this sort of history – as instructive, edifying, illuminating and equally horrifying, as it may be - isn't very useful in the Grand Schemes of any past or current avatar of the Big Bad Who. This is a history we are carefully programmed to consciously disremember: to collect, collate, stamp, file away with the rest of our amnesias, and plumb forget. Or just delete.

> [3] A shift in the structure of experience
> Told the farmer on his Andean plateau
> "Your way of life is obsolescent." –
> But hasn't that always been so?
> Anne Winters (*The Displaced of Capital*)

[4] *Honi Xuma* is an abbreviated form of *nixi honi xuma*, a name applied by Manuel Codova-Rios (in *The Wizard of the Upper Amazon*) to a sacred entheogenic drink used by The Baby Rookie's target, the Huni Kui. It's probably made from *banisteriopsis*, known in parts of the Amazon as *ayahuasca* – "the vine of the soul." It's used for personal healing, to set the soul to wandering, to communicate with spirits, and to merge with the collective in a common pool of thought, feeling and memory. The psychoactive principles are *beta-*

253

carbolines and *tryptamines.* **Honi Xuma** also lists as an indigenous word for headman, though I can't tell you in which language. **Mr. URUKUMU** said very little about this, beyond the fact that the mindless actions of The Baby Rookie and his Droogs in this respect are reprehensibly sacrilegious. Like pissing on the main altar in a Catholic church, defiling a Torah, Koran or Bible, or assassinating ArchBishop Oscar Romero while he's saying Mass. But we already knew that, didn't we?

⁵ *The following text montages various thoughts, ideas, quotes on political violence – which we have labelled, Terror, just to share a common sky of meaning. Most of this pertains to authoritarian versions of strong state imposed terror against other / weaker states, or against the strong state's own citizens. These are thoughts / opinions offered by theoreticians, pracitioners, fellow travelers, the dubious and opponents, alike. Some might call this a rant, and maybe it is; but I consider it merely additional information. These ideas and conjectures give us more context for understanding some of the social roots of the ontological core of The Baby Rookie's story. Or, at the very least, for formulating better, more useful questions. Because "after all is said and done, only major doubt keeps false truths and wonders at bay, as questions, questions, questions kiss the ashram: like bullets, back in the day."*

The Jacobin leader, Maximilian Robespierre, in a perfect expression of Enlightenment bi-polarity, claimed the basis for a popular government during a revolution is both virtue and terror. Because pure terror unleavened by virtue lacks any moral core and ultimately becomes baneful, and evil. But virtue without the force of terror is simply useless; it's terror that imbues virtue with power.

"Those who make Revolutions by halves do but dig their own graves."
     Louis-Antoine de Saint-Just

Both Robespierre and Saint-Just were prime movers in the Jacobin inspired Reign of Terror waged by the Revolutionary Committee

254

of Public Safety against alleged enemies of their version of the new French Revolutionary State. This Terror (both the state-imposed variety and freelance actions) left many thousands dead and ended in the Thermidorian Reaction against the campaign. Both of them were sent to the guillotine during the Reaction and the Terror ended, soon after. Both justified their use of Terror by appeal to French Revolutionary vigilance and patriotism, in light of how Revolutionary France was besieged by aggressive foreign monarchies, and their monarchistic operatives within France, itself. All of which was true.

Revolution Requires Less Moral Conscience: "Some of our comrades have too much mercy, not enough brutality, which means they are not so Marxist. On this matter, we have no conscience. Marxism is that brutal."
  Mao Zedong

This hard-edged "realist's" viewpoint applied equally well to the capitalist practice of *Realpolitiks*. With most of the emphasis on profit and any gestures toward ideology strictly there to grease the wheels. Like breaking eggs to make a rich, gooey omelette.

"A revolutionary class which has conquered power with arms in its hands is bound to, and will, suppress, rifle in hand, all attempts to tear the power out of its hands. Where it has against it a hostile army, it will oppose to it its own army. Where it is confronted with armed conspiracy, attempt at murder, or rising, it will hurl at the heads of its enemies an unsparing penalty."
  Leon Trotsky

"To overcome our enemies we must have our own socialist militarism. We must carry along with us 90 million out of the 100 million of Soviet Russia's population. As for the rest, we have nothing to say to them. They must be annihilated."

    Grigory Zinoviev

And Joseph Stalin viewed Terror as the perfect leverage for locking the discordant currents of individual desires and ideas into a collective tsunami of one weaponized, universal feeling, moving in a single direction, steered by fear and the will of a capable leader. He trained that weapon on his own people, initially (I guess) in the interests of building the New Soviet Person: a selflessly collective, norm-shattering, free and self-regulating exemplary being – among other things. This project obviously went clean off the rails and Terror morphed into a primary appendage of the Boss, the Big Bad Who: his needs, his appetite for control, his passion to crush his personal as well as ideological enemies in his paws of iron, and his raging paranoia. And some of the outcomes of this radical derailment: the Ukrainian *Holdomor*, the Soviet Gulag, all the long years of Great Terror.

Joseph Stalin personally supervised the assassination of Trotsky, and the trial and subsequent execution of Zinoviev, one of the original revolutionary Bolsheviks. This happened during Stalin's Great Terror.

Marx, the (I believe) unwitting progenitor of this whole strand of political theorizing, held that no one should ever be imprisoned for political or religious beliefs.

And Engels wrote to Marx on the subject of Terror in 1870: "Terror is to a great part useless cruelty, committed for the sake of their own reassurance by people, who are themselves afraid."

Stalin thought Engels gave the practical science of Terrorism a bad rap. He considered Marx, Engels, and Lenin to be genuine revolutionaries, but corrupted by capitalist / middle-class values. All of them weaned on Enlightenment concepts of humanism, ethics and morality. Fatally infected by early exposure to bourgeois prejudices. In essence, just too much conscience for the serious business of revolution.

Both Che and George Orwell have been described as "cross-border terrorists." Che's *Foco* theory centered on the uses of guerrilla forces to sap the will of fuedalistic capitalism in South America, and how poltically developed guerrillas must provide a nucleus for campesino-centered revolutionary movements. His guerrilla group in Bolivia ambushed and killed a number of national soldiers before he was captured and executed. Orwell was a participant (though admittedly minor) in partisan military operations to further the Republican cause, primarily, in Catalonia during the Spanish Civil War. Ambushes were made / individuals – both Nationalist soldiers and Fascist political thugs - were killed / and the seeds of useful fear, sown. But both Che and Orwell were uncomprisingly anti-authoritarian in their outlook and actions. How, then, should we judge them now? And who is fit to make that judgement?

But why are the examples of Terrorism we instinctly turn to in history drawn almost entirely from the radical revolutionary left and - very occasionally, if at all – from the authoritarian / Fascist right? That state-imposed Terror-ops by the NAZI's, the Soviet NKVD, Mao's Red Guard or the Khmer Rouge bob to the top is understandable: the extent and organized nature of the carnage was so staggering. On a lesser scale, the military regimes of Pinochet's Chile, the *Leaden Years* of Brazil's Junta, and Efrain Rios Montt's grip on Guatemala also belong in this "elite" club. (I'm staying close to home, there are so many more.) And why are leftwing grassroots insurgencies like Peruvian *Sendero Luminoso*, or the *Túpac Amaru Revolutionary Movement*, the Irish *Provos*, Palestinian *Fatah*, or the Indian Maoist *Naxalites* deemed more dangerous to society

257

than rightist groups like the "unofficially" U.S. financed Nicaraguan *Contras*, right-wing paramilitaries of various stripes throughout Central America, *Mascara Roja*, or the *Ulster Volunteer Force?* Are differences in core political / economic beliefs or comparative levels of violence the source of this view? Or is this all just because Fascism and Capitalism (aka: Authoritarian Terror and Profit) seem so inextricably joined at the hip?

I don't have an answer; I'm no historian, much less a political scientist. My tendencies toward praxis rather than theory have led me much closer to Paulo Freire and Augusto Boal that any real Marxist would ever admit. But for whatever reasons, Capitalism has been deemed more or less ethically-neutral and seems to get a pass in most of this discourse. Like this special breed of political / economic ideology would never stoop to using such a blunt and indiscrimimate set of levers as a means to realizing its hegemonic ends. Or wouldn't need to, based as it is (allegedly is) on natural market forces. So what's political about that?

Indigenous peoples find this view unintelligent and insulting, at best. The wide historical record, and their own personal and collective memory include a staggering array of Terroristic tactics employed by their European / Euro-American oppressor / usurpers, some more guileful and nuanced, some based on straight ahead Shock & Awe. From the first Entrada – armored conquistadors on horseback with guns, pikes and, cannon - to Lord Jeffrey Amherst and his bio-warfare plans for gifting the Seneca with smallpox-laden blankets (Seige of Fort Pitt / (now) Pittsburgh, Pennsylvania). To the Trail of Tears – based on Andrew Jackson's Indian Removal Act (1830) - which featured the forced march of Cherokee, Choctaw, Muscogee, Seminole and Chickasaw peoples from ancestral lands in the Southeastern United States to exile in the Oklahoma Territory. To the Long Walk of the **Diné** – under Kit Carson's baleful eye – to Bosque Redondo, New Mexico, for internment. To the Sand Creek Massacre of Cheyenne and Arapahoe women, children and old men in Colorado. To the

Hollister gun rapid-fire massacre of Spotted Elk's (aka Big Foot) Miniconjou-Hunkpapa band of Ghost Dancers at Wounded Knee, South Dakota: this list could go on almost indefinitely.

From first contact in the fifteenth century, to this very moment: millions of indigenous have been killed (with many still at risk) through contact with the white man's physical and mental diseases. While hundreds of thousands of others are killed in massacres or very unequal combat with the forces of Shock & Awe Terror in its early primitive, or later more nuanced, but equally lethal, manifestations.

And this Terror against indigenous peoples is more than fairly current. In fact, it's still happening on many continents.   In the decade between 1975 and the mid-80's, the U.S.-backed Guatemalan Armed Forces and various paramilitaries conducted 626 massacres, destroyed 440 Mayan villages, and killed 40,000 of which 83% were indigenous Mayan (re: Efrain Montt). Remember when we called the educational arm of our technical guidance, The School of the America? In 1997, *Mascara Roja* paramilitaries killed 45 members of the *Tzotzil* community in Acteal, Chiapas, Mexico. The current government of Jair Bolsonaro in Brazil has publically expressed its intention to suppress or eliminate its indigenous peoples to develop the Amazon rain forest with minimal interference. They claim this is their nation's Manifest Destiny, though not, precisely, in those words. I think we've heard that before, somewhere, no?

The still ongoing *EZLN* (Zapatista) Revolution that flowered as an (only initially) armed social justice struggle in Chiapas, Mexico, (1994) is a modern indigenous solution to this 500+ year (and counting) Reign of Terror. As such it warrants careful, unbiased study. And ongoing support.

While the Terror of the colonial enterprise may have begun in a monarchist / mercantilist format, it morphed into an increasingly modern capitalist (quasi-democratic) enterprise without missing a beat. Racism and economic exigency remained (and stiil remain) the major engines that steer the beast. Total domination is still the ultimate goal. The only discernable differences involve advances in lethal weaponry, legal sophistry, (sometimes) softer methods of cultural absorption, and unalloyed appropriaton of anything that's not nailed down. If tempting booty is, however, well attached: they merely pull the nails, cut it down, burn it to the ground, and sell what's left.

And we must remember, the multi-national slave-trade to the Americas was once considered just another species of ... well ... trade. Nothing but a piece of business, however distasteful, unsavory, brutally amoral and more. With its own specialized sectors for procurement / supply lines and logistics / delivery systems / inventory control / assessing macro/micro economic impacts on the worth of slaves and the overall costs of doing business. This system was, also, always managed through Terror. Owners did what they chose to enforce discipline and squeeze the useful life out of their property.

And the various slave-states enabled these acts with laws, and supported the owners with state force (slave patrols / official state militias). No questions asked. Always under the auspices of capitalism. For the good of the otherwise unsustainable gentleman-farmer agrarian economy (really nascent AgriBiz without the requisite machines, yet, to replace human labor). And after slavery was "officially abolished," Terror mechanisms like public lynching, convict labor / prison chain-gangs, and the Klan kept a lid on this grossly unequal, thoroughly racist, social dynamic in the former slave-holding states. Neutral, indeed.

[6] Marine Major General Smedley Butler commanded U.S. Marines in the Phillipines, China, Central America and the Caribbean (during the "Banana Wars"). He was widely acclaimed, received the Congressional Medal of Honor (twice), and at the time of his death

was America's most highly decorated soldier. He had an astute understanding of how the rarified world of Big Bad Who's works, and for whom it really works, and why. He once described his military service as " ... a career as a high-class muscleman for Big Business, for Wall Street, and for the Bankers." He wrote a book called *War Is a Racket.*

[7] From Franz Fanon's "Black Skin, White Masks"

CPSIA information can be obtained
at www.ICGtesting.com
Printed in the USA
LVHW041425251021
701485LV00022B/151